African Ethics and Death

This book analyzes the concepts of moral status and human dignity in African philosophy and applies them to the moral problems associated with death.

The book first challenges the criticism and rejection of moral status in African philosophy and then continues to consider how moral personhood is defined in African ethical theories, investigating which entities have full moral status or moral personhood and are therefore worthy of full ethical consideration. It then applies this theory to the problems associated with death. In the medical context, will an African theory of moral status permit or forbid euthanasia? Do we have moral obligations towards dead human bodies? Overall, the book provides an important African axiological contribution to debates on global ethics and moral philosophy.

Providing an important overview of the ethical problems associated with the biological fact of death, this book will be of interest to researchers across the fields of philosophy and African studies.

Motsamai Molefe is Senior Researcher, Centre for Leadership Ethics in Africa (CLEA), University of Fort Hare, South Africa, and Editor-in-Chief of the *South African Journal of Philosophy*.

Elphus Muade is an expert in medical ethics, medical law, environmental ethics, and bioethics with a PhD from the University of Kwazulu–Natal, South Africa. He is currently doing his post-doctoral fellowship at the Centre for Leadership Ethics in Africa, University of Fort Hare.

Routledge Studies in African Philosophy

Futurism and the African Imagination
Literature and Other Arts
Edited by Dike Okoro

Critical Conversations in African Philosophy
Asixoxe – Let's Talk
Edited by Alena Rettová, Benedetta Lanfranchi and Miriam Pahl

Environmental Justice in African Philosophy
Munamato Chemhuru

Feminist African Philosophy
Women and the Politics of Difference
Abosede Priscilla Ipadeola

Kimmerle's Intercultural Philosophy and Beyond
The Ongoing Quest for Epistemic Justice
Renate Schepen

African Epistemology
Essays on Being and Knowledge
Edited by Peter Aloysius Ikhane and Isaac E. Ukpokolo

African Ethics and Death
Moral Status and Human Dignity in Ubuntu Thinking
Motsamai Molefe and Elphus Muade

For more information about this series, please visit: www.routledge.com/Routledge-Studies-in-African-Philosophy/book-series/AFRPHIL

African Ethics and Death
Moral Status and Human Dignity in Ubuntu Thinking

**Motsamai Molefe
and Elphus Muade**

LONDON AND NEW YORK

First published 2024
by Routledge
4 Park Square, Milton Park, Abingdon, Oxon OX14 4RN

and by Routledge
605 Third Avenue, New York, NY 10158

Routledge is an imprint of the Taylor & Francis Group, an informa business

© 2024 Motsamai Molefe and Elphus Muade

The right of Motsamai Molefe and Elphus Muade to be identified as authors of this work has been asserted in accordance with sections 77 and 78 of the Copyright, Designs and Patents Act 1988.

All rights reserved. No part of this book may be reprinted or reproduced or utilised in any form or by any electronic, mechanical, or other means, now known or hereafter invented, including photocopying and recording, or in any information storage or retrieval system, without permission in writing from the publishers.

Trademark notice: Product or corporate names may be trademarks or registered trademarks, and are used only for identification and explanation without intent to infringe.

British Library Cataloguing-in-Publication Data
A catalogue record for this book is available from the British Library

ISBN: 978-1-032-65840-7 (hbk)
ISBN: 978-1-032-65846-9 (pbk)
ISBN: 978-1-032-65849-0 (ebk)

DOI: 10.4324/9781032658490

Typeset in Times New Roman
by Apex CoVantage, LLC

Contents

PART 1
African Moral Philosophy   1

1   Introduction to Moral Status and Death in African Ethics   3
2   A Defence of Moral Status in African Philosophy   18
3   Ubuntu Ethics, *ubuntu*, and Moral Status   40
4   Ubuntu, Empathy, and Moral Status   59

PART 2
African Applied Ethics   79

5   Ubuntu Ethics and Voluntary Euthanasia   81
6   Ubuntu Ethics and the Moral Status of Dead Human Bodies   97

Index   *111*

Part 1
African Moral Philosophy

1 Introduction to Moral Status and Death in African Ethics

Introduction

This book contributes to African moral philosophy, specifically in relation to the concepts of moral status and death. The concept of moral status is prominent in Western philosophy. It represents a particular method to value theory, where moral value is assigned to some entity relative to it possessing certain ontological attributes or capacities (Behrens, 2013).[1] Scholars in ethics use the term *moral status* to identify moral patients, that is, beings towards which moral agents have direct moral obligations. We may understand these obligations in both negative (not to harm moral patients) and positive (to benefit them) terms (Metz, 2012; DeGrazia, 2013). The book's first and primary aim involves ascertaining the place of the concept of moral status, the capacity-based approach to value, in African philosophy. We will be pursuing the question of whether a capacity-based approach to value (*qua* moral status) is compatible with African moral thought.

The book is as much about moral status as it is about human dignity in the literature in African philosophy. In this book, we use the concepts of moral status and human dignity interchangeably. To have human dignity amounts to having the highest degree of moral status, which scholars in the literature in ethics refer to as "full moral status" (FMS) or "moral personhood" (Kittay, 2005: 100; Jaworska & Tannenbaum, 2023: np). That is, among the community of those with moral status, some have it partially and others have it fully. Those who have it (moral status) fully have human dignity (Toscano, 2011). Often, we will use the concept of moral status unless in places where we specifically seek to refer to human dignity. We do so largely because the literature in African philosophy is less familiar with the language of moral status than it is with the language of human dignity. The book aims to put the spotlight on the concept, or the moral language, of moral status in African ethical theory.[2]

The second aim of the book concerns the moral issues occasioned by the biological fact of death. By "death", for purposes of this book, we limit our focus to the issues associated with (a) the process of dying that prompts

DOI: 10.4324/9781032658490-2

the moral question of euthanasia – the so-called end-of-life issues in bioethics (Schulman, 2008) – and (b) when a person dies, we are left with human remains – the dead body or cadaver. The question that confronts us involves determining whether dead human bodies count as objects of intrinsic value in their own rights. Put simply, the question involves evaluating whether dead human bodies do have moral status.

The first aim of the book involves the articulation and defence of the relevance of the concept of moral status (or human dignity) in African moral thought. We understand the first aim to involve a philosophical intervention on the *concept* and *conception* of moral status in the literature in African moral philosophy (Kymlicka, 1990.)[3] At the level of a concept, our intervention recognizes that there is a fundamental doubt among some scholars of African thought about the relevance of moral status (Menkiti, 1984; Tangwa, 2000). Given the scepticism or even the repudiation of the concept of moral status by some scholars of African thought, there is therefore an urgent need to clarify the nature of this concept and to argue for its place in African ethical theory. Even if scholars would converge on the suitability of the concept of moral status, that would not be where matters end. We still need to proceed to the level of a conception or theory of moral status.

At the level of conception or theory of moral status, we have the philosophical task to substantiate what it is (the relevant metaphysical feature) that grounds and explains why we have moral status or human dignity. In simple terms, at the level of theory, we aim to propose a novel conception of moral status and offer a preliminary defence of its plausibility in African philosophy. Hence, the first and primary aim of the book is to intervene at both conceptual and substantive levels concerning the relevance and importance of moral status in African ethical theory. The second aim of the book focuses on the problem of death. In relation to the second aim, we will apply the African theory of moral status to the issues associated with death: (a) euthanasia and (b) the moral standing of dead bodies.

Now that we have a sense of the aim of the book in relation to the concepts of moral status and death, the next section discusses the motivation of the book. To do so, it will employ two strategies. On the one hand, it will give the reader the sense of the status of the literature in relation to the relevant concepts and/or issues, and on the other hand, it will identify the gaps in the literature and suggest how it will tackle these deficiencies in the literature. The next section will consider two issues that we may classify under the rubric of methodology, namely, the question of how we understand and use the moniker "Africa" when we talk of the *African* theory of moral status, and we will specify the method we will use to pursue our aims in the book. The final section will proceed to discuss the structure of the book, where we will give the reader an overview of the chapters that constitute this book.

We turn now to the factors that motivate the relevance of this book.

The Motivation of the Book

Three reasons motivate the importance of the book, focusing on the concepts of moral status and death in African ethics. The first reason concerns the concept of moral status. The second reason involves the status of the debate on the plausible conception of moral status in African philosophy. The final reason pivots on the problem of death in African thought.

The Concept of Moral Status

The first reason that motivates the emergence of this book revolves around deficiencies in the literature on the concept of moral status in African philosophy. First, it is important to appreciate the growing body of literature focusing on the idea of moral status in African philosophy (Behrens, 2010, 2014; Metz, 2012, 2021; Chemhuru, 2016; Molefe, 2017, 2020; Oyowe, 2021; Atuire, 2022). Scholars have articulated the concept of moral status and have applied it to various practical contexts. Some have applied it to environmental ethics (Behrens, 2010; Chemhuru, 2016), others to animal ethics and marginal cases (Metz, 2012; Molefe, 2020), and others to questions of abortion (Molefe, 2022; Metz, 2021; Atuire, 2022), among others.

A close examination of the literature on moral status in African philosophy, however, reveals that it is plagued by a major deficiency. We note that there is a scepticism about the relevance of the idea of moral status in the literature in African philosophy. Influential scholars such as Ifeanyi Menkiti (1984), Godfrey Tangwa (1996), and Polycarp Ikuenobe (2017) have questioned the standard idea of moral status, or its method of assigning value, the capacity-based approach to value, in African philosophy. The major concern is that many of the scholars working on the idea of moral status proceed as if this scepticism or even rejection of the idea of moral status does not require a philosophical defence. The question involves whether moral status has a place in African ethical theory.

While it is important to recognize the contribution that scholars working in African thought are making on the idea of moral status, we think the scepticism cannot be simply swept under the carpet. If the engagements on the idea of moral status are to be robust, we, as scholars working on and with this idea, have an intellectual responsibility to respond to the scepticism towards it and justify the relevance of moral status in African philosophy. It is therefore quite concerning that scholars have not proffered a direct response to the rejection of moral status and argue for its plausibility.

In relation to this deficiency in the literature on moral status, we will offer a response and defence of the concept of moral status in the literature on African philosophy. One important reason that we believe it is crucial that we justify the relevance and place of the idea of moral status in African philosophy is to dispel the idea that this way of assigning value is essentially Western. We believe it is (or ought to be) a universal feature of ethics to assign value relative to the possession of certain metaphysical capacities, at least as part of a robust ethical system, without regard to whether it is African, Indian, or Asian. It is an accidental feature of the idea of moral status that has been predominant in the Western tradition of philosophy (Molefe, 2020).

A Conception (or Theory) of Moral Status

The second reason that motivates the emergence of the book involves the competing theories of moral status in African philosophy. Some of the theories of moral status take ethical supernaturalism as their meta-ethical point of departure, where they prescribe a religious ontological feature as the basis for it (Wiredu, 1996; Bujo, 2001; Ilesanmi, 2001; Bikopo & van Bogaert, 2009; Molefe & Maraghanedzha, 2022). Those who subscribe to ethical supernaturalism tend to prescribe the spiritual property of vitality, life, or even *okra* (soul) as the basis for moral status (Gyekye, 1992, 1995; Kasenene, 1998; Bujo, 2001; Iroegbu, 2005). Some scholars take ethical naturalism as a point of departure, where they prescribe some physical ontological property as the basis for moral status. Some account for it in terms of the capacity for friendliness, the capacity for sympathy, or merely being a member of the human community (Menkiti, 1984; Tutu, 1999; Metz, 2012; Molefe, 2019). In relation to the second motivation, the reader should note the two following considerations.

In terms of the divergence between ethical supernaturalism and naturalism in African ethics, the book presumes the latter meta-ethical position as a plausible understanding of African ethics. That is, we will stipulate ethical naturalism as the most promising moral view in African ethics. We stipulate this position because many scholars working in African ethics tend to construe it as embodying ethical naturalism. Often, scholars of African thought describe ethical naturalism in terms of *ethical humanism*, which involves identifying some ontological property of our human nature as the basis for morality (Wiredu, 1992; Gyekye, 1995, 2010; Okeja, 2013; Molefe, 2015; Metz, 2021).[4] The book will concentrate on those accounts of moral status that operate based on ethical naturalism. Our stipulation and preference for ethical naturalism do not preclude the possibility of a meaningful debate about ethical naturalism and supernaturalism in African philosophy for those interested in such a project. The debate concerning which view between the two meta-ethical positions is plausible lies outside the scope of this book. We intend to contribute to secular views on moral status and the problems associated with death in African philosophy.

We clarify the intervention the book will make towards debates on a plausible theory of moral status. The reader should note that scholars posit different theories of moral status, but they have not made it their project to survey the emerging and extant accounts of moral status in the literature and proceed to defend one of them as the most plausible. A recent paper by Caesar Alimsinya Atuire (2022), "African Perspectives of Moral Status: a Framework for Evaluating Global Bioethical Issues", exemplifies this tendency in the literature. The paper promises to give the global community of philosophy African perspectives on moral status. In our view, the paper does not live up to its promises to provide a global framework for evaluating bioethical issues. The paper does not give the reader a sense of why the idea of moral status is important and relevant in African ethics. This kind of clarification and defence of the concept of moral status is important, given the growing rejection of the relevance of the idea of moral status in ethics and bioethics in the Western tradition (Macklin, 2003; Blumenthal-Barby, 2023). It does not give the reader an overview of the emerging and extant theories of moral status in African ethics. Finally, even the moral account of moral status it articulates remains untested in terms of its plausibility, and it is not clear how it can contribute to global bioethical issues.

To give the reader a sense of how the book will contribute to the debates on moral status, we consider important axiological concepts that will constitute our plausible account of moral status in African ethics. Scholars working on African ethics, specifically in the debates on moral status and human dignity, tend to rely on the ideas of *ubuntu* and/or personhood (Behrens, 2010; Metz, 2012; Chemhuru, 2016; Ikuenobe, 2017). We will also rely on these concepts. We use the concepts of *ubuntu* and/or personhood interchangeably. We draw the distinction between Ubuntu and *ubuntu*.[5] The former (Ubuntu) refers to a system of philosophy as a whole associated with the Bantu people spread across southern, eastern, and central Africa (Eze, 2005; LenkaBula, 2009). For example, one can speak of German philosophy, which refers to the general patterns or features of German thought. In relation to Bantu people, the term *Ubuntu*, in its capitalized form, represents their philosophical system that embodies its own metaphysics, epistemology, and axiology (Ramose, 1999). Ubuntu, as an axiological system, prescribes the achievement of *ubuntu* or personhood as the chief moral goal.

Ubuntu ethics prescribes *ubuntu* as the final good. The concept of *ubuntu* embodies a virtue-oriented moral perfectionism, which requires the agent to cultivate a virtuous disposition (Wall, 2012). To have *ubuntu* means that the agent has a virtuous character (Tutu, 1999; Menkiti, 2004; Molefe, 2019). One major theoretical contribution we will make involves interpreting *ubuntu* as the final good in terms of empathy. It is the concept of *ubuntu* or empathy, as the final good, that we will use to construct an African theory of moral status, where we will account for it in terms of the capacity for empathy. We will offer the reader *prima facie* reasons to take seriously the empathy-based interpretation of African ethics by comparing it with the prominent account of it in the literature of Ubuntu, the friendliness view of *ubuntu*.

Applied Ethics and the Problem of Death

The scarcity of literature focusing on the relationship between ethics and death in African ethics motivates the emergence of this book. We identify two areas of philosophical interest associated with death. One will struggle to find philosophical accounts focusing on the problem of euthanasia in African ethics. The etymology of the word "euthanasia" signals mercy killing or a good death. That is, in a medical context, a competent medical practitioner permits or actively terminates the patient's life for her own benefit, which is a function of relieving the patient from endless and pointless suffering (Foot, 1977). In the literature, one will find expressions of the prevalent moral intuitions in African thought that tend to consider it permissible (Tangwa, 1996; Bikopo & van Bogaert, 2009). One will, however, struggle to find a systematic exposition of African ethics, specifically the idea of moral status and its application to the problem of euthanasia (Tangwa, 1996; Bujo, 2001). Molefe (2020) and Metz (2021) have recently written chapters in their monographs that focused on euthanasia. These two works make important contributions to African bioethics, but we will add an underexplored empathy-based justification of the permissibility of euthanasia in African thought.

The second problem relates to the moral status of dead human bodies. Do dead human bodies have moral status? Alternatively, do we have moral obligations towards dead bodies? This question remains generally neglected in the literature on African philosophy (Muade, 2021). Some scholars outrightly reject that dead human bodies have moral status (DeGrazia & Millum, 2021), and some scholars believe that they do have it (Rosen, 2012). In the African tradition, Thaddeus Metz (2012) operates with the moral intuition that dead bodies do have moral status. The book emerges to respond to the scant literature in relation to the question of the moral status of dead human bodies.

We draw largely from African thought, specifically Ubuntu thinking, to reflect on this question. We will ultimately argue that dead bodies do not have moral status. We pursue this question for two important reasons. First, it teaches us something crucial about the assumptions of dominant moral theories. One such insight assumption is that prominent moral theories posit properties that only imagine living human beings as proper objects morality – consider properties such as well-being, capabilities, autonomy, *ubuntu*, and so on. Second, this question is important in that it has practical implications for the bioethical question concerning the use of cadavers in medical research and training. Is it permissible to use dead bodies for training and research in medicine?

We turn next to methodological issues.

Methodological Issues

In what follows, we consider two methodological issues. First, we clarify the use of the word "African" in the context of articulating an African moral theory. Second, we clarify the method we will use to defend our views.

The Moniker African

To explain the term *Africa*, we draw from Mogobe Ramose's adumbrations on it. Ramose (2003), in the essay titled "I doubt, therefore African philosophy exists", discusses the origins and meaning of the term *Africa* in the context of clarifying the nature of African philosophy. In terms of the origins of the term *Africa*, Ramose (2003: 118) avers, "It has emerged in the course of our considerations above that the term 'African' is of Greek and Roman origin. It does not arise from the indigenous conquered inhabitants of the continent (Africa)". The Western onlooker in the continent gave the name Africa to indicate the weather conditions of this place: sunny or no cold weather. The term *Africa*, Ramose argues, does not bear or make any specific reference to the peoples of the place or anything significant about their cultures. If Ramose's adumbrations are true that at least the name "African" does not come from peoples from this place, does it follow that we should jettison it?

Ramose does not believe that we should do so. In fact, he proposes that we have a duty to embrace the name and to give content to it. He considers this project an urgent and an ethical one. Ramose (2003: 118) argues that it is not necessary to jettison the term *Africa*. Instead, he proposes that we retain the term but remain aware of the moral and political duties associated with making this choice. He considers this important ethical and political exercise to be a *struggle for reason*. This project has both negative and positive components. The negative project involves resisting and repudiating all impositions from external sources that seek to degrade humanity and place Africa. Note that we do not resist all possible contributions or positive appropriations that arise in mutual exchanges as cultures intersect and interact. We reject meaningless and arbitrary impositions in our quest to (re)define Africa. The positive project involves the most important cultural, moral, and political project of self-determination, where the peoples of Africa deliberate, decide, and collaborate on the project of building their own future in their own terms.

The retention of the term *Africa* must be necessarily divorced from the tendency to romanticize it. The romantic view of Africa tends to believe that everything in precolonial Africa was perfect and beautiful. In fact, it tends to essentialize what could simply be thought to be contingencies (tendencies) as essential features of what it means to be African. This romantic picture of Africa tends to operate with a homogenizing, simplistic, and often dehumanizing picture of African peoples. When we talk of "Africa", we think of it as a place like any other in the world characterized by all things that human beings can do. A place where there were/are kingdoms, moments of peace and of wars, different approaches to deal with economic issues, marriage, burials, and so on (Wiredu, 2008). These are features of any and every society, although their form may differ from one culture. On our part, we are not committed to any kind of unjustified essentialism in regard to Africa and what it means to be African. The term *Africa* captures the intersection of thought and place that we interpret to represent moments for possibilities (creativity) in our continued engagements about defining ourselves. In this sense, the content of this term will always have a contested dimension, as we debate from our different vantage points the kind of meaning we can associate with it. Remember, Ramose (2002) construes the journey of self-determination for Africans as "a *struggle* for reason".

With this background, we can draw from the literature the starting point to reflect and construct the meaning of the term *Africa* that is operational in this book. Scholars of African thought define the term *Africa*, at least plausible uses of it, in two related ways (Metz, 2007a, 2007b; Oyowe, 2014; Ikuenobe, 2016). Oritsegbubemi Oyowe (2014: 333) explains the two meanings of the term *Africa* in this fashion: "One picks out a geographical category merely while the other refers to a family of ideas distinctive of cultures in the geographical area denoted as Africa". The term *Africa*, in the first instance, refers to a place occupied by a people with its own experiences, history, and cultures. One can identify a place in the map. The second meaning of the term relates to "a family of ideas distinctive of cultures" in the place. The point of the second component that explains the meaning of Africa requires us to recognize that as much as Africa is characterized by diversity and heterogeneity, it also has certain common or salient themes, which Oyowe refers to as a "family of ideas distinctive" to Africa.

Another influential scholar of African thought, Thaddeus Metz (2010: 52), identifies the following as an example of the basket of ideas distinctive to Africa:

> Indigenous sub-Saharans often think that society should be akin to family; they typically refer to people outside the nuclear family with titles such as "sisi" and "mama"; they tend to believe in the moral importance of greetings, even to strangers; they normally think that there is some obligation to wed and procreate; they generally say that "charity begins at home" or that "family comes first"; they frequently believe that ritual and tradition have a certain degree of moral significance; they usually do not believe that retribution is a proper aim of criminal justice, inclining toward reconciliation; they commonly think that there is a strong duty for the rich to aid the poor; and they often value consensus in decision-making, seeking unanimous agreement and not resting content with majority rule. I have the space merely to suggest that these recurrent values are plausibly entailed and well explained by the prescription to respect relationships in which people both share a way of life and care for one another's quality of life.

To say these ideas are "distinctive" in/to Africa does not mean that they occur everywhere in Africa and solely in it; rather, it denotes their prominence in Africa rather than in other places (Metz, 2007). On our part, we will be using the idea of *Africa* to refer to both a place and the family of ideas salient in it.

Remember, we noted that we will construct an African perspective of moral status from Ubuntu ethics, which refers to a salient philosophical and axiological system among African cultures (Eze, 2005; LenkaBula, 2009).[6]

African Analytical Philosophy

Now that we have clarified how we use the term *Africa*, we proceed to consider the method we will use to conduct our philosophical inquiry in the book. The book belongs to the body of work that contributes to African analytical philosophy. This means that we use the techniques of analytic philosophy in the context of African philosophy (Wiredu, 1980, 1996; Gyekye, 1995, 1997; Matolino, 2014, 2019; Molefe, 2019, 2021; Oyowe, 2021; Metz, 2021). Two features characterize the analytic technique of philosophy, namely, conceptual analysis and argument (Dower, 2014). We make sense of the world and much of the content we explore in it, in the search for meaning and truth, by use of language, or specifically concepts. In this sense, concepts serve as essential resources in our search for meaning and truth. Linguistic or conceptual analysis requires us to break down concepts to their basic elements so that we can understand, define, and use them properly in our intellectual engagement on issues.

Without a proper use and understanding of concepts, we may never be clear about the problem, and our search for theoretical solutions may be a chimera. Gyekye (1992: 242–243) speaks on this wisdom concerning conceptual analysis in the context of African philosophy:

In times of wonder and uncertainty, in times when the definition and articulation of values and goals become most urgent, in times when the search for fundamental principles of human activity becomes most pressing and is seen as the way to dispel confusions and unclarities, the services of philosophy become indispensable. Philosophy is a conceptual response to the problems posed in any given epoch for a given society. It is therefore appropriate, even imperative, for contemporary African philosophers to grapple at the conceptual level with the problems and issues of their times, not least of which are the problems of government and political stability.

Gyekye construes philosophy as a conceptual response whose major service involves dispelling confusions and unclarities. We dispel confusion and uncertainty because the aim of a philosophical discourse involves a correct grasp and use of concepts to respond to issues before us. If the concept of Ubuntu is central in our search for the values and goals it espouses for a decent society, then philosophy as a conceptual response would involve breaking this concept into constituent elements to understand it correctly and clearly define it and to further deploy it to make sense of the moral world.

Philosophizing does not end at merely being clear and precise in our understanding and use of language and concepts. Often, it also involves or even requires that we argue or defend particular views as true or better when compared to others. Justifying or arguing for the validity or soundness of certain claims or theses falls under the rubric of what we call an *argument*. The function of an argument pivots on providing reasons that certain claims/views ought to be taken seriously or are plausible and why we ought to reject others since they lack rational credibility. The measure of plausibility is a function of the weight of reasons that buttress a certain view. The stronger the weight of reasons, which serve as evidence, then the more plausible the view under consideration. If the reasons supporting a particular view are weak, then we may not take the claim/view seriously or as valid or even sound. Philosophers rely on reasons as the standard of acceptability of claims or views. The quality of reasons determines the validity of claims/views. Metz (2007: 378) exemplifies how plausibility (via a quality of reason) works in the analytic tradition:

> The method of positing a general principle, posing a particular counterexample, reformulating the general principle to avoid the counterexample, posing a new counterexample to the reformulated principle, revising the principle yet again, and so on. That is the kind of methodology I have in mind when I speak of seeking to achieve my aim in a "systematic, analytic way".

The method of establishing the validity of claims/views/principles via reason is measured by the quality of reason/evidence that supports it. The less a principle/view is able to stand up to counterexamples, the weaker it is, largely because of the lack of quality of the reasons that buttress it. However, if the principle or view is able to respond adequately to counterexamples, then it is secured by strong reasons.

In this light, we can conclude by noting that analytic philosophy demands that we be clear regarding the use of language and concepts so that we can properly understand the questions and issues before us. It also requires that we provide reasons (as evidence) for the claims or views that we propose or defend. It is one thing to have a clear understanding of the concept of God and quite another thing to provide reasons for the existence of God. On our part, we will use the analytic technique of philosophy to clarify and defend the relevance of the concept and conception of moral status in African ethics.[7] Our defence of an empathy-based interpretation of Ubuntu thinking in relation to moral status will, at best, be preliminary in that it will be inviting scholars in African philosophy to seriously consider a sentimentalist interpretation of African ethics, which posits empathy as foundational.

In what follows, we consider the structure of the book.

The Structure of the Book

The structure of the book tracks its dual aims, the theoretical and practical contributions to African moral philosophy. The theoretical component focuses on the concept and conception of moral status in African philosophy. The applied component focuses on the moral issues associated with death. The theoretical component will do three things in relation to the concept of moral status: (a) it will identify the scepticism against the idea of moral status (Chapter 2); (b) it will offer reasons that we should not take the scepticism seriously (Chapter 2); and (c) it will articulate an Ubuntu-based account of moral status (Chapter 3) and offer a preliminary defence of an empathy-based account of moral status (Chapter 4). The second component, the applied section of the book, focuses on two moral issues associated with death, namely, (d) euthanasia (Chapter 5) and (e) the moral status of dead human bodies (Chapter 6).

The next chapter articulates an Ubuntu-based account of moral status.

Notes

1 Generally, we will, as a matter of convenience, use *capacities* or *attributes* in the plural. This does not mean that we are not aware of ethical monism or pluralism, where either a moral theorist posits a single capacity or several of them.
2 In Chapter 2, we clarify the relation between moral status and human dignity.
3 I draw to the attention of the reader the distinction between a *concept* and a *conception*. The first one refers to an abstract idea of a thing (moral status), and the other refers to our theoretical substantiation of it, to give content to it. It is one thing to have the concept of moral status and quite another what it is in virtue if we have it (Kymlicka, 1990).
4 *Ethical naturalism* is open about what physical thing can serve as the meta-ethical basis for morality. That is, any natural object can serve as the basis for morality. The common interpretation of the ethical naturalism in African philosophy identifies human nature, hence, humanism, as the preferred meta-ethical view in African philosophy (Gyekye, 2010).
5 We are not the first ones to draw the distinction between Ubuntu and *ubuntu*. Leonhard Praeg (2014), in his prolific book *A Report on Ubuntu*, adumbrates one way to make sense of this distinction. On his view, the capitalized Ubuntu refers to a precolonial conception of African ethics, which, for reasons connected to colonialism, we can never recover. On the other hand, *ubuntu*, the noncapitalized expression of it, refers to the various interpretations of it available in the literature.
6 The fact that our approach draws from ideas that are salient in African philosophy does not necessarily imply that we will not draw from useful and relevant ideas from other traditions (Gyekye, 1995). We do not imagine a proper approach to African philosophy as one that requires exclusive reliance on intellectual and axiological resources from Africa. We do believe, however, that there is a need for theorizing or philosophizing that foregrounds African thought and ideas, and hence, this project contributes to African philosophy as gateway to contribute to global thought.

7 We are aware that some may object that the analytic technique of philosophy is Western, and if we are to pursue a true project of "African" philosophy, then we have to use an African method (whatever the objector may consider as a true African method). Two reasons support why we insist on the analytic techniques of philosophizing. The first just is the *corpus* of literature that uses it in African philosophy. We are aware that this is not the only method of doing African philosophy, but we will add our voices in it along those in the field that prefer and use analytic philosophy. The second reason is the intuitive appeal inherent in the techniques of analytic philosophy. The idea of properly using language and concepts to represent and understand issues is common among all cultures. If we do not do linguistic or conceptual analysis, how shall we be clear and precise on matters or questions before us? Moreover, the requirement to provide reasons or justify our claims or positions are universal to all cultures. Surely, if ours is a struggle for reason, it does imply that we are committed to reason as a standard of validity or truth. In this sense, the use of language and argument as a proper form of engagement is ultimately a human activity of pursuing and defending validity or truth. It is a contingent feature of it that it emerged in a particular form in the Western tradition, or so we believe.

References

Atuire, C. (2022). African Perspectives of Moral Status: A Framework for Evaluating Global Bioethical Issues. *Medical Humanities* 48: 238–245.

Behrens, K. G. (2010). Exploring African Holism with Respect to the Environment. *Environmental Values* 19: 465–484.

Behrens, K. G. (2013). Two 'Normative' Conceptions of Personhood. *Quest* 25: 103–119.

Behrens, K. G. (2014). An African Relational Environmentalism and Moral Considerability. *Environmental Ethics* 36: 63–82.

Bikopo, D., & van Bogaert, L. J. (2009). Reflection on Euthanasia: Western and African Ntomba Perspectives on the Death of a King. *Developing World Bioethics* 10: 42–48.

Blumenthal-Barby, J. (2023). The End of Personhood. *The American Journal of Bioethics*. DOI: 10.1080/15265161.2022.2160515.

Bujo, B. (2001). *Foundations of an African Ethic: Beyond the Universal Claims of Western Morality*. New York: Crossroad Publishing.

Chemhuru, M. (2016). *The Import of African Ontology for Environmental Ethics*. Johannesburg: University of Johannesburg.

DeGrazia, D. (2013). Equal Consideration and Unequal Moral Status. *The Southern Journal of Philosophy*, 31: 17–31.

DeGrazia, D., & Millum, J. (2021). Moral Status. In *A Theory of Bioethics*. Cambridge: Cambridge University Press, 175–213.

Dower, N. (2008). The nature and scope of development ethics. *Journal of Global Ethics* 4:183–193.

Eze, O. (2005). Ubuntu: A Communitarian Response to Liberal Individualism. *Masters Dissertation*. Pretoria: University of Pretoria.

Foot, P. *Euthanasia. Philosophy & Public Affairs* 6: 85–112.

Gyekye, K. (1992). Person and Community in Akan Thought. In K. Gyekye & K. Wiredu (Eds.), *Ghanaian Philosophical Thought Studies*, vol. 1. Washington, DC: Council for Research in Values and Philosophy, 101–122.

Gyekye, K. (1995). *An Essay on African Philosophical Thought: The Akan Conceptual Scheme*. Philadelphia: Temple University Press.

Gyekye, K. (1997). *Tradition and Modernity*. New York: Oxford University Press.

Gyekye, K. (2010). African Ethics. In E. N. Zalta (Ed.), *The Stanford Encyclopedia of Philosophy*. http://plato.stanford.edu/archives/fall2011/entries/african-ethics (accessed 16 January 2013).

Ikuenobe, P. (2016). The Communal Basis for Moral Dignity: An African Perspective. *Philosophical Papers* 45: 437–469.

Ikuenobe, P. (2017). The Communal Basis for Moral Dignity: An African Perspective. *Philosophical Papers* 45: 437–469.

Ilesanmi, O. (2001). Human Rights Discourse in Modern Africa: A Comparative Religious Perspective. *Journal of Religious Ethics* 23: 293–320.

Iroegbu, P. (2005). Do All Persons Have a Right to Life? In P. Iroegbu & A. Echekwube (Eds.), *Kpim of Morality Ethics: General, Special and Professional* (pp. 78–83). Ibadan: Heinemann Educational Books.

Jaworska, A., & Tannenbaum, J. (2019). The Grounds of Moral Status. In E. Zalta (Ed.), *The Stanford Encyclopedia of Philosophy*. https://plato.stanford.edu/entries/groundsmoral-status/ (accessed 14 February 2023).

Kasenene, P. (1998). *Religious Ethics in Africa*. Kampala: Fountain Publishers.

Kittay, E. (2005). Equality, dignity and disability. In: Waldron A, Lyons F (Eds.), *Perspectives on equality: the second Seamus Heaney lectures*. Liffey, Dublin, pp. 95–122.

Kymlicka, W. (1990). *Contemporary Political Philosophy: An Introduction*. Oxford: Clarendon Press.

LenkaBula, P. (2008). Beyond anthropocentricity-Botho/Ubuntu and the quest for economic and ecological justice. *Religion & Theology* 15: 375–394.

Macklin, R. (2003). Dignity is a useless concept. *BMJ* 327: 1419–1420.

Matolino, B. (2014). *Personhood in African Philosophy*. Pietermaritzburg: Cluster Publications.

Matolino, B. (2018). *Consensus as Democracy in Africa*. NISC (Pty) Ltd.

Menkiti, I. (1984). Person and Community in African Traditional Thought. In R. A. Wright (Ed.), *African Philosophy: An Introduction*. Lanham: University Press of America, 171–181.

Menkiti, I. (2004). On the Normative Conception of a Person. In K. Wiredu (Ed.), *Companion to African Philosophy*. Oxford: Blackwell Publishing, 324–331.

Metz, T. (2007a). Toward an African Moral Theory. The Journal of Political Philosophy 15: 321–341.

Metz, T. (2007b). Ubuntu as a Moral Theory: Reply to Four Critics, South African Journal of Philosophy 26: 369–387.

Metz, T. (2010). Human Dignity, Capital Punishment and an African Moral Theory: Toward a New Philosophy of Human Rights. *Journal of Human Rights* 9: 81–99.

Metz, T. (2012). An African Theory of Moral Status: A Relational Alternative to Individualism and Holism. *Ethical Theory and Moral Practice: An International Forum*, 14: 387–402.

Metz, T. (2021). *A Relational Moral Theory: African Ethics in and Beyond the Continent*. Oxford: Oxford University Press.

Molefe, M. (2015). A Rejection of Humanism in African Moral Tradition. *Theoria* 62: 59–77.
Molefe, M. (2017). A Critique of Thad Metz's African Theory of Moral Status. *South African Journal of Philosophy* 36: 195–205.
Molefe, M. (2019). *An African Philosophy of Personhood, Morality and Politics*. New York: Palgrave Macmillan.
Molefe, M. (2020). *An African Ethics of Personhood and Bioethics: A Reflection on Abortion and Euthanasia*. New York: Palgrave Macmillan.
Molefe, M. (2022). *Human Dignity in African Philosophy: A Very Short Introduction*. Cham: Springer.
Molefe, M., & Maraganedzha, M. (2023). African Traditional Religion and moral philosophy. *Religious Studies* 59: 355–367.
Muade, E. (2021). Towards a Theory of Moral Status of the Dead and its Contribution to Medical Research and Learning: The Case of Unclaimed Cadavers. [Dissertation]. Pietermaritzburg: UKZN.
Okeja, U. (2013). *Normative Justification of a Global Ethic: A Perspective from African Philosophy*. New York: Lexington Books.
Oyowe, A. (2014). Fiction, Culture and the Concept of a Person. *Research in African Literatures* 45, 42–62.
Oyowe, A. (2021). *Menkiti's Moral Man*. Lanham, Md: Lexington Books.
Praeg, L. (2014). *A Report on Ubuntu*. Pietermaritzburg: University of KwaZulu of Press.
Ramose, M. (1999). *African Philosophy through Ubuntu*. Harare: Mond Books.
Ramose, M. (2002). *African Philosophy Through Ubuntu*. Harare, Zimbabwe: Mond Books Publishers.
Ramose, M. (2003). I Doubt, Therefore African Philosophy Exists. *South African Journal of Philosophy* 22: 113–127.
Rosen, M. (2012). *Dignity: Its History and Meaning*. Cambridge, MA: Harvard University Press.
Schulman, A. (2008). Bioethics and the Question of Human Dignity. In *The President's Council on Bioethics, Human Dignity and Bioethics: Essays Commissioned by the President's Council*. Washington, DC: President's Council on Bioethics, 2–19.
Tangwa, G. (1996). Bioethics: An African Perspective. *Bioethics* 10: 183–200.
The Ethics of Need: Agency, Dignity and Obligation. New York: Routledge.
Tangwa, G. (2000). The Traditional African Perception of a Person: Some Implications for Bioethics. *Hastings Center Report* 30: 39–43.
Toscano, M. (2011). Human Dignity as High Moral Status. *The Ethics Forum*, 6(2): 4–25.
Tutu, D. (1999). *No Future Without Forgiveness*. New York: Random House.
Wall, S. (2012). Perfectionism in moral and political philosophy. In: Zalta, E. (Ed.). *The Stanford encyclopedia of philosophy*. http://plato.stanford.edu/archives/win2012/entries/perfectionismmoral/.
Wiredu, K. (1980). *Philosophy and an African Culture*. Cambridge: Cambridge University Press.
Wiredu, K. (1992). Moral foundations of an African culture. In: Wiredu, K., Gyekye, K. (Eds.), Person and community: Ghanaian philosophical studies, 1. *The Council for Research in Values and Philosophy*, Washington, DC, pp 192–206.

Wiredu, K. (1996). *Cultural Universals and Particulars: An African Perspective.* Indianapolis: Indiana University Press.
Wiredu, K. (2008). Social Philosophy in Postcolonial Africa: Some Preliminaries Concerning Communalism and Communitarianism. *South African Journal of Philosophy* 27: 332–339.

2 A Defence of Moral Status in African Philosophy

Introduction

The chapter ascertains the place of moral status in African ethical theory. It evaluates the suitability of the method of assigning value to moral objects associated with the concept of moral status. Roughly, the idea of "moral status" identifies objects of direct moral obligation or moral patients (DeGrazia, 2013). Generally, the concept of moral status assigns value to things relative to whether they possess the relevant ontological features. Things that possess the relevant ontological capacities count as members of the moral community or as moral citizens (or patients). The question about the relevance of moral status in African philosophy is motivated by some scholars' scepticism of the relevance of moral status and its method of assigning value in African philosophy. The chapter defends the relevance of moral status in African ethics, or Ubuntu thinking. The argument will suggest that *constraints, egalitarianism,* and *human rights*, which are moral concepts associated with moral status, render it an indispensable component of any robust ethical framework.

To defend the relevance of moral status in African philosophy, the chapter will proceed as follows. The first section considers the concept of moral status. The second section expounds on the scepticism and/or rejection of moral status in African philosophy. Finally, we provide two reasons that justify why we must take the concept of moral status seriously. The moral concepts of constraints, egalitarianism, and human rights provide a strong ground for why we must not jettison moral status in African philosophy.

We begin with the concept of moral status.

The Concept of Moral Status

Given that the chapter (and book) is about moral status, we start by considering it. We provide a general picture of moral status as a concept which we believe or hope most scholars will consider acceptable. Our aim is not to contribute to the literature by defending the most plausible definition of *moral status*. We aim to give the reader a sense of this concept and go on to defend its relevance in African philosophy. Moreover, we limit the scope of our focus to moral status as a method of assigning or attributing value to things, that is, the value-ascribing function (of moral status) is the prime focus of this book. We will identify the following elements associated with moral status: (a) it provides the standard of morality that defines how we should identify moral patients and the duties that moral agents have towards them; (b) we will also distinguish between the concept and a conception of moral status; (c) we distinguish between two frameworks to interpret a theory of moral status: moral individualism and relationalism; and (d) we clarify the relationship between moral status and human dignity.

Defining Moral Status

Moral status specifies the moral agents' obligations towards moral patients. In moral theory, we distinguish between *moral agents* and *moral patients* (Sen, 2001). *Moral agents* are those that act or ought to act directed by the demands of morality. *Moral patients*, on the other hand, are those things towards whom we have moral duties or obligations, recipients of moral actions. Typically, moral patients are vulnerable to things that moral agents can do to harm, degrade, or undermine them. The idea of a moral agent signifies an actor who has moral duties toward others, and the idea of a moral patient signifies the ones acted upon whom morality requires that we regard and consider when we act towards them. The idea of moral status imposes direct duties on moral agents in relation to moral patients. Hence, the idea of moral status is a *moral patiency* – at least that is how we understand it.

Note that the obligations that arise for moral agents towards beings that have moral status are *direct* in their nature, that is, these duties arise in relation to them (moral patients), and these duties are owed to them in their own right. For example, when a person breaks my chair, they have not done something wrong to the chair, since it is not a moral patient, that is, the chair does not "bear direct or independent moral importance" (DeGrazia, 2008: 182). The wrong done involves the owner of the chair that bears direct and independent moral importance. In the case of the chair, the duty not to break it is indirect or dependent; the agent should not break the chair to respect the owner. That is, the agent has a direct duty towards the owner and an indirect duty towards the chair.

For some beings, to have moral status denotes that agents have direct obligations towards it because it is morally significant. Things can go wrong towards a being with moral status in two related ways. On the one hand, when we act amiss towards a being of moral status, we are violating a moral principle, that is, the act itself counts as wrong since it fails to live up to the standards of morality. The morality inherent in the idea of moral status defines how we ought to act towards a being with it (the moral patient), and when we fail to do so, we have acted wrongly. On the other hand, when we act amiss towards a being with moral status, we not only break a moral law, merely *doing* something wrong, but in a way of speaking, we are also "breaking" the being itself, that is, we are violating or harming it (Metz, 2012). The idea of moral status captures both facets of how things can go amiss in relation to a moral patient. We can act *wrongly* (objectively, we are failing to live up to the standards of morality), and we *wrong* (harm, degrade it, and undermine it) the being itself. Rape illustrates the two ways things can go amiss in relation to moral status. The act violates a moral principle and harms the victim by degrading her humanity.

Now understand that the idea of moral status identifies beings towards which we have direct obligations. The next question we should consider involves how the idea of moral status defines the standard of morality. The concept of moral status generally accounts for the standard of morality, or value, by appealing to certain significant ontological attributes or capacities of a thing. That is, a thing that has the relevant ontological capacity does have moral status, and nothing that does not possess the relevant capacity has moral status. In other words, the idea of moral status is one that assigns value by considering whether the thing does possess the relevant ontological capacities.

The abortion debate can illustrate how moral status accounts for the standard of morality. The debate on abortion pivots on the idea of moral status, that is, whether a foetus does have moral status (Hursthouse, 2013). Scholars operating with ethical supernaturalism, a religious approach to ethics, would prescribe the metaphysical capacity of a soul, or *imago dei*, as the standard for morality (Schroeder & Bani-Sadr, 2017). In this view, the mere possession of the soul, or *imago dei*, is necessary and sufficient for moral status. Ethical naturalists prescribe various physical features, such as the human genetic make-up or the potential for cognitive abilities or consciousness, as the basis for morality (Warren, 1997; Behrens, 2013). If the possession of consciousness or self-awareness serves as the basis for moral status, then it would follow that a foetus does not have it. Hence, abortion would be permissible on this view.

The following considerations stand out about the idea of moral status, particularly as an approach to assigning value. First, some object has moral status, or value, if and only if it possesses the relevant ontological capacity. The mere possession of the ontological capacity amounts to the being under consideration having intrinsic value. That is, it has moral value in its own right because of the kind of thing that it is (Korsgaard, 1983; Sulmasy, 2009). The value is intrinsic precisely because it possesses what is considered value-endowing capacity, be it consciousness, rational, a soul, or whatever else a theorist may propose as a suitable ontological capacity. Our obligations, as moral agents, emerge in relation to the value-endowing capacity of the object in question.

Second, the mere possession of a certain capacity makes being inherently valuable. In other words, the value and obligations arising in response to it, which (value) arise because of certain ontological capacities, have nothing to do with how well or bad the agent uses them (the capacities) or the extent to which it has the relevant capacity (Hughes, 2011). That is, the value encapsulated by the idea of moral status is independent of the use (whether positive or negative) of the capacities. One has value merely because she has the capacity; hence, this concept is a patient-centred (or even the capacity-based) notion of value rather than an agent-centred one (Behrens, 2013). A hardened criminal has moral status because she possesses the relevant ontological capacity. Since moral status is the kind of value that is a function of the kind of thing the entity is, it should follow that we do not acquire it. Hence, it is not given, it cannot be taken away, and we cannot lose, so long as we continue to have the relevant metaphysical make-up (Toscano, 2011; Miller, 2017).

A Concept and Conception of Moral Status

Moral status defines morality or assigns intrinsic value relative to the thing's ontological make-up or capacities. Hence, we observe that the idea of moral status embodies a capacity-based approach to value in as far as it assigns (intrinsic) value to things relative to whether they possess the relevant ontological capacity (Hursthouse, 2013). The difference between a concept and a conception (or theory) of moral status resides in that the latter (theorists) propose different ontological capacities to account for moral status (Metz, 2012). The concept of moral status identifies beings towards which agents have moral obligations, whereas a theory of moral status offers the substantive ground that specifies the relevant ontological capacity that accounts for moral status (Jaworska & Tannenbaum, 2019). Kantians identify the ability to think (sophisticated cognitive abilities), capabilities approaches (basic capabilities), and care ethics (the capacity to care) as the relevant ontological capacity as the ground for moral status (Singer, 2009; Nussbaum, 2011; Miller, 2017).

Moral Individualism and Relationalism

Different theories of moral status are packaged differently – some individualistic, and others relational. Individualistic theories of moral status assign it by virtue of a certain characteristic feature(s) of a thing (May, 2014). Wassermann *et al.* (2017) note that individualistic theories of moral status tend to appeal to the following internal characteristic(s) of a thing to account for it:

> These accounts [individualistic accounts of moral status] identify overlapping clusters of psychological and cognitive attributes – self-consciousness, awareness of and concern for oneself as a temporally extended subject; practical rationality, rational agency, or autonomy; moral responsibility; a capacity to recognize other selves and to be motivated to justify one's actions to them; [and] the capacity to be held, and hold others, morally accountable.

Influential theories of moral status or human dignity in the Western tradition of philosophy – Kantianism, utilitarianism, contractualism, capabilities approaches – tend to be individualistic in that they account for it by appeal to one or more of these internal features of an entity.

Relational accounts of moral status, on the other hand, do not just focus on the location of the capacity that is internal to a thing when defining it, but they tend to emphasize its functional orientation to connect with others. In this sense, the relational approach to moral status tends to account for moral status in terms of the capacity to relate or connect with others. Examples of relational approaches to moral status cite the capacity to care or love as its basis (Miller, 2017; Metz, 2021). It is not the actual caring or loving relationship that confers moral status; it is mere capacity for it that does. The common element between the individualist and relational approaches to assigning moral status is that they both locate it in some capacity (or characteristic) of our nature, the individualist aspect. The difference, however, lies in that, on the former, the relational feature is merely contingent, and on the latter, it is essential to account for moral status.

The Relation between Moral Status and Human Dignity

Another crucial consideration in relation to the concept of moral status, at least as we understand it in this book, is that it comes in degrees (DeGrazia, 2008). Some things in the world do not have moral status at all, but among those that have it, within a continuum of gradations in terms of degrees, others have none of it, some have it partially, and others fully. A weak anthropocentric interpretation of ethics, for example, assigns full moral status to human beings and only partial status to animals (Molefe, 2020). Metz (2012) argues that we should consider the idea of moral status as admitting degrees since this way of rendering it allows us to be able to resolve trade-off cases. Consider a trade-off case where one must choose between saving a rat or a human being. Although we may believe that both have moral status, we must save a human being over the rat because the latter has greater moral status than the former.

Manuel Toscano (2011) defends the claim that moral status comes in degrees by appealing to what he calls *Waldron's hypothesis*. Toscano provides a useful way to explain the relation between moral status and human dignity. Central to Jeremy Waldron's (2009) intervention on the concept of human dignity is the observation that the best way to understand it is in terms of the concept of status. The move to construe human dignity in terms of status has a historical basis in the evolution of the term *dignity* in European history (Rosen, 2012). Waldron observes that the idea of human dignity, the traditional concept associated with ancient Roman society, had two elements. The first element of human dignity is that it is hierarchical, and the second element is that it is associated with high rank or nobility. To have dignity is to have a high status, or rank, and those who occupy the high rank are associated or analogized with nobility. Waldron (2009: 2016, emphasis mine) explains this view of human dignity in this fashion:

> However, it will also generate an account of it as noble bearing and an account of the importance of the ban on humiliating and degrading treatment. That is what I am trying to do with an account of dignity as a high-ranking status, comparable to a rank of nobility – *only a rank assigned now to every human person, equally without discrimination: dignity as nobility for the common man.*

Toscano's strategy to explain the relation between moral status and human dignity, drawing from Waldron, involves construing human dignity as a high status, which he associates or analogizes with the rank of nobility. Unlike in antiquity, the modern notion of human dignity now accommodates or elevates everyone to this high status of nobility. To have dignity involves occupying a high moral status, which ranks now accommodate all human beings.

It is the insight of considering human dignity as a high-ranking status of nobility that Tuscany refers to as Waldron's hypothesis. Toscano invokes the hypothesis because its appeal to the idea of *status* allows us to understand that the notion of moral status, as in moral *status*, is open to degrees, where some have lower and others have higher status – the hierarchical element. In this light, to have human dignity amounts to the claim that human beings have the highest degree of moral status, which in the literature is also captured in terms of "full moral status" (Jaworska & Tannenbaum, 2019: np). Hence, we note that the idea of human dignity is tantamount to the idea of moral status, except that to have human dignity indicates that one occupies the highest status of value possible. The higher a being is in the hierarchy, the more morally significant it is. Thus, to have human dignity means that the being matters more than all other beings in the hierarchy of moral statuses that occupy lower levels of it in the hierarchy. Different things (species) occupy different levels in the hierarchy of value, as captured by their differing moral statuses, and human beings have human dignity because they occupy the highest position in the hierarchy.

To clarify the logic behind the idea of moral status as coming in degrees, Toscano (2011: 16) further notes:

> An explanation of human dignity as a moral status . . . is properly understood as a threshold concept, not a scalar one. As such, moral status is ascribed to a group of beings because of certain features they possess, regardless of the lesser or greater degree to which such beings have them. Reaching a threshold, i.e., being in possession of certain traits or features is a sufficient condition for having the appropriate status. Assigned on the basis of the relevant properties, X has (or does not have) a certain status, but X cannot have more or less of it. Therefore, there are no scales or

degrees in the enjoyment of status. A completely different thing is that beings with different features enjoy different moral statuses. As noted before, we use the notion assuming that there may be a plurality of statuses. Furthermore, to grasp human dignity as moral status, we assume that there must be a hierarchy within the plurality of moral statuses, arranging beings in higher or lower ranks because of their features. Therefore, the scale exists between different types of status but not within them.

Moral status is a threshold and a range concept. Given that moral status is an idea that we understand in terms of a hierarchy, it implies that there are different moral statuses (strata), depending on where the being is located on the hierarchy of value. The position of a thing on the hierarchy is determined by whether it has the relevant ontological capacity, which is necessary and sufficient for moral status on that particular position in the hierarchy. Anything that has the relevant property, say, rationality, meets the threshold or minimum standard, has moral status. As a range concept, the idea of moral status assigns some or equal moral status to anything that meets the threshold, without regard to how far above the minimum it is. Note the explanation for the range aspect of moral status:

> All beings that fall within the "range" – that reach the threshold level of the attribute – have the same moral status regardless of how far they exceed that threshold. (The term "range concept" comes from Rawls; his example is of points within a circle, all of which are equally "inside" despite varying distances from the circumference.)
>
> (Wasserman, 2017: n.p.)

The idea is that when a being has the relevant capacity, or at least meets the minimum threshold, it has the same moral status as any other being in the moral circumference, without regard to its actual position within it. To have human dignity, one simply needs to meet the minimum requirements of the highest moral status in the hierarchy.

It is also crucial to note the important clarification offered by Tuscany regarding scales in our understanding of moral status. Each sphere/stratum of moral status in the hierarchy has its own threshold (and range). To be a part of a particular sphere (or stratum) of moral status in the hierarchy, one needs simply to meet the minimum threshold, which will allow them to have the same moral status as the things in that sphere. The crucial point to appreciate here is that scales do not apply within a particular sphere of moral status; they only apply across different strata/spheres of moral statuses in the hierarchy. If we have rationality as the standard of moral status, for example, then anything that meets the minimum threshold has full moral status – in this case, we may have human beings. Gorillas, given that they have some rationality, may not necessarily meet the threshold for full moral status, but they may have their own sphere of moral status below that of human beings. If, for example, dolphins and elephants meet the threshold of the sphere associated with gorillas, then they belong to the same sphere and have the same moral status as do gorillas. If there are other beings that meet another threshold below that of dolphins, then they will occupy a lower sphere of moral status than that of human beings and dolphins, and so on.[1]

This section considered the idea of moral status. Moral status identifies moral patients, beings towards which agents have moral obligations. The duties we owe to entities with moral status are direct or owed to them for their own sake. We distinguished between the concept (the abstract idea) and a conception (or theory) of moral status. We further noted that a theory of moral status can either be individualistic or relational. We concluded by noting that the idea of moral status admits degrees, which has helped us understand the relation between moral status and human dignity. The idea of degrees has helped us to also understand the idea of moral status as both a threshold and range concept. Now that we have a sense of the idea of moral status, we can turn to the scepticism towards the idea of moral status in African philosophy.

Scepticism and Rejection of Moral Status

To outline the scepticism towards the idea of moral status in the literature in African philosophy, we will focus on the writings of four scholars, Kevin Behrens, Ifeanyi Menkiti, Godfrey Tangwa, and Polycarp Ikuenobe. In a very powerful essay, "The Two Normative Conceptions of Personhood", Kevin Behrens (2013) distinguishes two normative concepts of personhood. He associates one concept of personhood with African philosophy and another with Western philosophy. He associates African approaches to value theory with the agent-centred notion of personhood, which assigns value strictly in terms of the quality of the agent's performance. That is, the salient concept of personhood in African philosophy, or approach to value, is meritorious in nature in that it assigns value relative to the quality of the agent's conduct or character. Hence, he associates the African concept of personhood with a perfectionist approach to ethics, which engenders the agent to realize her true nature by nurturing virtue or excellence.

On the other hand, he associates the Western approach with the patient-centred notion of a person, which assigns value relative to the mere possession of certain ontological capacities. He observes that the patient-centred notion of personhood prevalent in the Western tradition of philosophy is "related to the notion of moral status" (2013: 107). He further notes that on this view of personhood, value is assigned relative to possessing "the necessary capabilities or properties" that define who counts as a moral patient. He proceeds to observe that different theorists posit different ontological properties for moral status or moral personhood in this fashion – "[s]ome theorists set the bar very high requiring self-consciousness . . . sentience, reasoning, self-directed activity, communication and/or self-awareness" (ibid.).

The purpose of Behrens's essay alerts scholars working in African and Western philosophy of the two distinct approaches to value theory or moral personhood, where one approach places emphasis on the agent and her conduct as the site of value and another places it on the patient and the possession of certain ontological capacity as the site of value. On the African approach, value arises relative to actions, and on the Western approach, it arises relative to possessing certain capacities.

Considering the distinction between the African and Western approaches to value, provide an outline of the scepticism or even rejection of the idea of moral status, or the capacity-based approaches. Tangwa (1996: 126), one of the leading bioethicists in African philosophy, comments as follows in relation to the patient-centred (or capacity-based approach to value):

> [T]he morality of an action or procedure is to be determined from the standpoint of the agent rather than that of the patient (the recipient of action). . . . What the attributes of self-consciousness, rationality, and freedom of choice do . . . is load the heavy burden of moral liability, culpability, and responsibility on the shoulders of their possessor. Human persons are not morally *special*; they are morally *liable*.

Tangwa is aware of the distinction between the patient- and agent-centred approaches to value. According to Tangwa, we have to approach morality from the standpoint of the agent and not the patient. Tangwa insists that the possession of certain ontological capacities does not render human persons morally special; rather, it renders them morally liable. The reader should note that the idea of being morally special is associated with the idea of moral status, where the moral patient is special merely because she possesses the relevant ontological capacities. The specialness at play here is a function of her being intrinsically valuable, which value tracks her ontological capacities. On Tangwa's view, or at least our reading of him, the mere possession of a certain ontological capacity renders moral agents merely morally liable, and moral liability engenders duties for the agent to develop and use her capacities positively. To recognize these capacities is to assume responsibility, as an agent, to duly develop and use them correctly; it is only in the context of using these capacities positively that moral specialness can emerge.

The same scepticism regarding moral status, or the capacity-based approach to morality, is present in Ifeanyi Menkiti's interpretation of personhood and value theory. Wiredu credits Menkiti for being the first scholar to explicate the normative concept of personhood in African philosophy, which Behrens describes as the agent-centred notion of personhood (Wiredu, 2004, 2009; Molefe, 2020). Menkiti notes the distinction between the Western and African concepts of personhood (and value). He describes the Western concept of a person as minimalistic in its approach to ethics because it explains a person (or value) solely in terms of possessing certain ontological capacities, such as a "soul, or rationality, or will, or memory" (Menkiti, 1984: 172). He describes the African view of personhood as *maximalist*:

> Insofar as it reaches for something beyond such minimalist requirements as the presence of consciousness, memory, will, soul, rationality, or mental function. The project of being or becoming persons, it is believed, is a truly serious project that stretches beyond the raw capacities of the isolated individual, and it is a project that is laden with the possibility of triumph but also of failure.
> (2004: 326)

The dichotomy between the minimalist and maximalist approaches not only serves to distinguish these two concepts of a person (or value), but it seems that Menkiti also uses it to criticize the former. In his view, the minimalist approach fails to give a correct approach to understanding moral value in ethical theory. In the same vein as Tangwa, Menkiti remains baffled concerning how the mere possession of rationality could render us morally special in any sense. The maximalist approach, on the other hand, at least according to Menkiti, construes value to emerge in the context of the agent and her conduct. The agent has to recognize that her most important project involves converting the raw capacities of her nature to be an embodiment of moral triumph and not failure. Menkiti construes triumph in terms of "ingathering of excellences" so that the agent can become a "bearer of norms" or to have the "full complement of excellences seen as definitive of the person" (2004: 326).

In light of the exposition of Behren's, Tangwa's, and Menkiti's approach to personhood and morality, we note the emergence of two ideas. First, we note the distinction (as noted by Behrens) between the patient- and agent-centred approaches to value, where he associates the former with Western philosophy and the latter with the African tradition. Second, we saw this dichotomy playing itself out in Tangwa's and Menkiti's scepticism towards the capacity-based approach to value. At the heart of this scepticism is the idea that moral value arises only in contexts of the activities of the agent and not merely the possession of certain capacities. The possession of capacities merely renders us morally liable, or they engender duties for agents to develop and use these capacities positively for the betterment of the community and ourselves as agents, which is the hallmark of communitarian ethics.

Following Tangwa's and Menkiti's scepticism towards the idea of moral status, Ikuenobe (2017, 2018), in the context of articulating an African conception of moral status (or human dignity) and human rights, also rejects the claim that the mere possession of capacities bears intrinsic value. We interpret Ikuenobe to provide a substantive account of Menkiti's idea of personhood as a maximalist approach to personhood or value theory. Ikueonobe sets himself to defend an African conception of moral status (or human dignity). Two central elements, at least in our view, constitute his account of moral status. The first and most important element is that his accounts associate ontological capacities strictly with instrumental value. The second element is that he explains human dignity (or moral status) entirely in terms of the meritorious notion of personhood, the agent-centred notion of it. The logic of his view, at least in our representation of it, flows as follows: ontological capacities have no intrinsic value but instrumental value, and "intrinsic value" emerges only in relation to the quality of our actions and characters.

Ikuenobe draws a distinction between the ontological and normative concepts of personhood. The former refers to the descriptive features that constitute human nature, such as the body and whatever else we may believe composes it. The ontological or descriptive sense of personhood is important because it identifies the capacities of our nature. The normative notion of person identifies moral agents that have done well in as far as they have been able to acquire or nurture virtue. Note that there is a relationship between the ontological and normative notions of personhood (Ikuenobe, 2015, 2016; Molefe, 2019, 2020). We read Ikuenobe to suggest that it is the development of the former (or the relevant capacities of our nature) that leads to the emergence of the latter (a virtuous character). That is, normative personhood (virtue) emerges relative to the development or positive use of the descriptive capacities of our nature.

Furthermore, Ikuenobe uses the distinction between the ontological and normative concepts of personhood to distinguish between *factual* and *moral dignity*. The mere possession of ontological capacities accords one factual dignity. He comments as follows regarding factual dignity:

> The descriptive sense may involve spiritual, metaphysical, or psychological facts, capacities, or *features that all humans have* or something they are innately endowed with by God. This is the sense in which people talk about all humans *having dignity*. One has a factually descriptive sense of dignity just in case one has vitality, life, soul, breathe, or spirit, and the capacity for cognition, rationality, autonomy, choice, agency, relationships, and communal belonging.
>
> (Ikuenobe, 2017: 457, emphasis mine)

The mere possession of ontological capacities, construed in physical or spiritual terms, merely secures factual dignity, a universal property possessed by all human beings. Notice that dignity is described as *factual* to indicate that it does not confer any intrinsic value. At best, ontological capacities, at least according to Ikuenobe, confer only instrumental value. He opines:

> *It is my view that human capacities are only an instrumental good*; they are only means for good life, choices, and actions that manifest respect for self and others, caring, mutuality and harmonious relationships. It is to be used productively as a contributory member of a community that makes one's good life and choices possible.
>
> (2017: 461)

It is in light of associating instrumental value with capacities that Ikuenobe insists that "moral dignity", as opposed to factual dignity, is a function of achieving personhood. Concerning moral dignity, Ikuenobe (2017: 457) opines, "Moral dignity involves a normative evaluative judgment about someone based on the moral quality of her character, achievement, comportment, or behaviour". Moral dignity refers to the kind of value that arises in contexts of actions that are meritorious. Moral dignity refers to the agent's achievement that reflects the quality of actions, dispositions, and character in the communal context. We can observe that the normative idea of personhood is tantamount to moral dignity. To achieve personhood, that is, to have a virtuous disposition, amounts to having moral dignity. Morality, or intrinsic value, in the truest sense, according to Ikuenobe, arises only in contexts of action and performance that positively develop and express the agent's ontological capacities.

In summary, in the analysis of the works of the four scholars of African moral thought, we noted the difference between two distinct approaches to personhood (or value theory), the agent-centred and the patient-centred (or capacity-based) approaches. The former accounts for value in terms of performance, and the latter accounts for value in terms of the positive use of the ontological to secure a virtuous character. We three influential scholars of Africa thought that disputing the capacity can bear intrinsic value, which we understand to be tantamount to rejecting the idea of moral status. They recognize the agent-centred approach to be the only plausible interpretation of African ethics, or Ubuntu thinking.

Next, we defend the capacity-based approach to value.

A Defence of Moral Status

We defend the capacity-based approach to value theory associated with moral status (or human dignity) in two related ways. The first defence outlines what is missing in an approach to ethics that jettisons the capacity-based approach to value. Alternatively, and more accurately, we identify the moral-theoretical deficiencies of the agent-centred approach to value theory when we espouse it on its own without the capacity-based approach as its foundation. The second line of defence takes a positive approach by considering the emergence and importance of human rights as a powerful philosophical and practical consequence of a capacity-based approach to value theory.

To make our first argument, we consider two cases that we believe that agent-centred approaches to value have moral-theoretical difficulties to satisfactorily account for. The first case involves protection from harm and/or our duties towards candidates who cannot use their capacities for various reasons. The second challenge involves accounting for moral egalitarianism, the moral and political idea of recognizing and treating citizens or moral patients as equals or equally.

The Case of Candidates That Cannot Use Their Capacities

The agent-centred theory of value has difficulties accounting for *constraints* or the idea that some things ought not to be harmed, interfered with, or violated. In a standard capacity-based approach, constraints (the moral reasons forbidding us from interfering with or harming a being) arise precisely because the entity is intrinsically valuable (Jaworska & Tannenbaum, 2019). Habermas (2010: 465) explains constraints associated with human dignity as follows: "The respect for the dignity of every person forbids the state to dispose of any individual merely as a means to another end, even if that end be to save the lives of many other people". Feder Eva Kittay (2005: 101) explains constraints in this manner: "Because of the properties that lend dignity to the group, certain things must not be done to *any* member of that group". The intrinsic value, or moral status or human dignity, is a function of the properties or capacities that lend dignity to that community of beings. That is, to recognize a thing for the kind of a thing that it is (its significant ontological capacities) embodies obligations for the agent not to harm it, all things being equal, without regard to the positive social and political consequences of meting out such a harm.

These constraints are a function of respecting the being of moral status or human dignity. Stephen Darwall (1977) defines the respect associated with respecting a thing for the kind of thing that it is as *recognition respect*. Recognition respect tracks the ontological capacities of a thing. Recognition respect embodies both negative and positive duties. That is, we will not harm a being merely because it possesses certain significant capacities. Moreover, we will aid it or empower it because it possesses certain ontological capacities. Our moral actions of respect and empowerment, as agents, track the ontological capacities and nothing else. The challenge arises immediately for the agent-centred view because it does not seem to have something like recognition respect. In fact, it is correct to associate personhood or agent-centred theories of value with Darwall's (1977) *appraisal respect*, which refers to respect that tracks outstanding performances or achievements.

Remember, the agent-centred approach does not consider capacities to have intrinsic value. Moreover, intrinsic value arises only in contexts of positive use of capacities. The agent-centred approach to value appears to fail to explain the inviolability or the protection that we owe certain candidates, particularly those without moral dignity. Consider the cases of foetuses, children before the age of reason, and marginal cases. All these candidates have the common property of not being able to exercise their capacities or to pursue personhood or moral dignity. If moral dignity, or moral value, arises only in contexts of positive performance, how do we satisfactorily account for our negative duties towards beings that cannot use their capacities? The agent-centred approach, at least the ones we are considering here, explicitly rejects the claim that a capacity or even potentiality might have moral value;

(intrinsic) value is a function entirely of positive use of capacities. It is not entirely clear how a merit-based account of value may account for our duties to protect vulnerable candidates such as infants, mentally incapacitated persons, and animals in their own right, since the question of value does not even begin to arise in relation to them, because they cannot use their capacities that are the only ground for intrinsic value.

One option for the agent-centred notion might involve offering indirect protections. We all know that appealing to indirect consideration is not a satisfactory explanation for why we ought to protect children and severely mentally injured persons. It sets a very low standard for why we ought to care and to protect them. A robust approach to morality surely ought to offer a stronger case for our duties towards children and severely mentally injured persons, which ought to involve respecting them for their own sakes. A satisfactory rationale is one that attempts to offer direct protection. We argue that the capacity-based approach seems well able to offer a direct account for why we ought to protect children, since they have the relevant capacity, at least possess the potential for it, or belong to the group typically associated with the relevant capacity (Gyekye, 1992).

Ikuenobe (2017: 464) provides another reason agent-centred theory may be deployed to account for our duties towards children and those with mental disability in this fashion:

> My view implies that we have unconditional responsibility to respect, love and care for those (children, those with mental or physical disability) who lack the ability to use their capacity to earn respect. The idea of respecting unconditionally those who are *not capable* of acting to earn respect is supported by the moral principle of "ought implies can", which indicates that you cannot hold people responsible for what is impossible for them.

The explanation for why we owe unconditional respect to candidates who cannot use their capacities, such as children and mentally disabled persons, is less than satisfactory. In fact, we find it to be completely beside the point. The real point that needs an explanation is not the uncontested claim that we cannot hold people responsible for what they cannot do. The real issue pivots on how we justify unconditional respect towards children and mentally disabled persons when all value or respect emerges on the condition of the positive use of capacities. If capacities merely have instrumental value, it means their value emerges in contexts of positive and relevant function; where these capacities cannot function, they have neither instrumental nor intrinsic value, which begs the question as to what is the source and basis for the unconditional respect Ikuenobe associates with children and marginal cases. The capacity-based approach locates value in the capacities themselves, or their potential or standing of some entity in relation to the capacity either historically possessing it or being a member of the kind that possess the relevant capacity (we suggest this line of reasoning in Chapter 4 in relation to the case of those who are severely mentally disabled). In one way or another, the capacity-based approach can or does have resources to explain our duties towards these candidates. The agent-centred approach does not seem to have resources to explain our duties towards candidates since they do not meet what it specifies as the standard of value – the positive use of capacities.

The force of this objection seems to highlight several related issues. Consider first the concern that the agent-centred theory seems to fail to offer a robust account of who counts as a moral patient. Or more accurately, it seems to controversially limit the scope of moral patients to those that can be moral agents. As a result, leaving out a host of many candidates that may not be moral agents, we tend to hold the intuition that includes them in the moral community – children, severely mentally incapacitated individuals, for example. As things stand, there is the challenge of explaining and justifying the source of our moral actions or responsibilities in general and towards specifically the candidates that cannot use their capacities.

Notice, in one place, Ikuenobe (2017: 452, emphasis mine) opines, "On this view, we have responsibilities to ourselves, others, communal relationships not necessarily because they have rights, but because *such responsibilities are simply the reasonable thing to do*". It cannot be that the sources of our moral responsibilities are accounted simply in terms of them being reasonable. If we use reasonability as the standard for our moral responsibilities, we have not yet answered the question of the source of these responsibilities; we have simply shifted the goal posts – what is to count as a reasonable thing to do? A promising explanation, if Ikuenobe is to be consistent, has to revolve around the instrumental value associated with our capacities. The basis should be that our responsibilities involve empowering others to pursue moral dignity. This explanation goes somewhere, but it does not go far enough in that it still leaves out those who lack these capacities or cannot use them in the first place that we intuitively believe that we have duties towards them, like children and those who are mentally impaired.

Furthermore, to appreciate the inadequacy of the agent-centred approach to explain the source of our responsibilities, consider the case of animal ethics. Animals present an interesting example of candidates that cannot exercise their capacities, particularly if the relevant capacities are personhood-oriented. There is a persistent moral intuition that we do have some duties towards animals, and the standard answer from the literature is that these duties emerge because animals do have certain natural or morally significant ontological capacities. The prominent feature that scholars across different ethical schools cite is that of sentience – the ability to suffer (Regan, 1985; Korsgaard, 1996; Singer, 2009). The agent-centred theory, on the face of it, does not have resources to account for our duties towards animals, given that value arises only in contexts connected to achieving personhood. It is not clear how the maximalist account can accommodate animals in the moral community in their own right. The indirect defence or protection of animals will not constitute a robust approach to animal ethics.

A robust ethical account must be able to explain the moral evil associated with certain ways of treating animals. Yes, it might not be good for an agent to be cruel towards animals, as that might undermine her own character. This kind of explanation, however, still says nothing about the duties and respect that we should have towards the animals in their own right. There are ways that our conduct can make the lives of animals worse off in terms of their quality of life. Our conduct towards animals, or any sentient being, for that matter, should be motivated by its own good without regard to ourselves in terms of our characters or quality of humanity in the first place, particularly if our aim is a robust animal ethics. The standard for the duties we owe towards animals should not be what is good for human beings, or at least that should not be the primary consideration. The primary consideration ought to be what is good for the animals themselves. The capacity-based approaches promise to offer this kind of explanation because it invokes the animal and its capacities as the basis for our obligations towards them, which the agent-centred theory, at least the ones we considered here, does not seem to have the moral-theoretical resources to accommodate them in the moral community.

We next consider the case of moral equality.

The Case of Moral Egalitarianism

One of the attractive features of the capacity-based approach to value à la moral status is that it offers a promising way to construct moral egalitarianism. The idea of egalitarianism, at least as we understand it here, involves recognizing the equality of moral patients or being able to account for it. The idea of equality operational here is that of moral equality among moral patients. The idea of moral status accounts for moral equality in terms of the mere possession of certain capacities. The mere possession of the invariant ontological capacity accounts for the equality of moral patients. Note that equality is a function of the mere capacity itself and not of its use. If we discover that two entities have the relevant capacity to the minimum threshold, on that basis alone, we can accord them equality. In this very sketch of a capacity-based approach, we obtain a sense of how it deals with the question of equality. Equality tracks are a function of merely possessing the relevant ontological feature.

The agent-centred approach seems to have a challenge in accounting for moral egalitarianism. Remember that agent-centred approaches account for value relative to the variant property of merit or performance. In the moral spectrum of moral dignity, we must reckon with the fact that we will have variable performances, where some agents will do worse than others and others will do better than others will. Performance, or merit, does not seem to be a stable moral property to ground or secure the value of equality. The moral insight of the modern approach to human dignity grounds it on a specific capacity to equalize everyone. Leading scholars of moral status (or human dignity) explain the relation between it and equality in this fashion: "the modern notion of *human* dignity involves an upwards *equalization* of rank, so that we now try to accord to every human being something of the dignity, rank, and expectation of respect that was formerly accorded to nobility" (Waldron, 2009: 229, emphasis mine). Michael Rosen (2012: 8, emphasis on mine) explains the relation between moral status and equality as follows:

> One very common way in which writers present the history of dignity is as part of what I call an "expanding circle" narrative. From this perspective, the quality of dignity, once the property of a social elite, has, like the idea of rights, been extended outwards and downwards until it has come to apply to all human beings. This is all part of that great, long process by which *the fundamental equality of human beings* has come to be generally accepted.

Waldron and Rosen observe that one of the outcomes of the evolution of the idea of human dignity from the traditional to the modern concept involves its ability to account for equality among moral patients. Historically, the traditional concept of human dignity – *dignitas* – referred to a status that was enjoyed by the elite or those that occupied nobility or high rank in society. *Dignitas* was positional- or rank-based. The privileges, duties, and rights associated with *dignitas* were a reserve of the few in society, while the commoners were excluded from the political package associated with this rank. The modern notion of human dignity has at least two crucial elements, as already alluded to in our discussion of the concept of moral status earlier. The first element is that it retains the hierarchical element from the traditional concept of human dignity, where it associates human dignity and the high rank of nobility. The second element drops the hierarchy at as it pertains to human beings, and instead, it democratizes the idea of human dignity, where dignity is a universal feature of every human being. There is no longer a distinction between the elites and the commoners; rather, we have everyone occupy the same and equally high status of human dignity. Hence, Rosen is correct to observe that the evolution of the idea of human dignity resulted in "the fundamental equality of human beings" because all human beings occupy the same (high) rank or status.

Scholars usually associate the status of human dignity with the property of being human. Historically, the traditional concept of human dignity grounded the status of human dignity on the human capacity for reason (Rosen, 2012). It is because human beings have particular ontological endowments that they enjoy the superlative status of human dignity. The idea of human dignity, at least salient interpretations of it, accounts for it in terms of certain capacities. Hence, the evolution of the idea of human dignity has the moral-political advantage of being able to offer a robust account of moral egalitarianism. Equality among moral patients is a function of merely possessing certain ontological capacities, which account for their intrinsic value and the equal status they enjoy in the political comity.

The moral-theoretical advantages of the capacity-based approach to value raise serious concerns in relation to the agent-centred approaches to account for equality. The agential features of the maximalist or personhood-based accounts of moral status (or moral dignity) do not seem suitable to account for the idea of equality among human beings. The major challenge is the variable nature of the ethical concepts or values associated with the agent-centred approaches to value, where the capacity-based approach promises to secure equality among moral agents by merely possessing the relevant property.

Human Dignity and Human Rights in Modern Politics

The second argument for the defence of moral status relies on the idea of human rights. Modern moral, legal, and political contexts are organized around the insight that human beings are morally special, and this moral specialness requires recognition, protection, and empowerment. The moral specialness of human beings finds expression through the relationship between human dignity and human rights. The Universal Declaration of Human Rights (1948), which serves as the modern moral-legal standard of a new world civilization, brings to the fore the importance of human dignity and human rights (Donnelly, 2009). The UNDR (1048) states, "All human beings are born free and equal in dignity and rights". There are at least two ways to conceive the relationship between human dignity and human rights: foundationalist and anti-foundationalist approaches (Freeman, 1995). The influential approach in the literature can be associated with the foundationalist approach to human dignity and human rights.

We will use the foundationalist approach to argue for the importance of capacities in the human-dignity-and-rights modern political culture. On the foundational approach to the relationship between human dignity and human rights, the former is primary, and the latter secondary. Jack Donnelly (2009: 1) captures this view as follows: "Human dignity is the foundational concept of the global human rights regime, 'the "ultimate value" that gives coherence to human rights'". Human dignity signifies the moral worth that states, its subsidiary agents, and citizens should recognize and respect. Human rights signify the moral, legal, and political strategies for expressing respect due to human dignity. Individuals with dignity must live under dignified conditions, and human rights specify the conditions of such decent or acceptable standards of human existence (Griffin, 2008; Donnelly, 2009).

We may not necessarily agree with the idea of human rights; however, we invoke it here to make a case about the importance of the capacity-based approach to value. We also recognize that the Universal Declaration of

Human Rights does not explicitly specify which capacity of human nature accounts for our human dignity (see Schachter, 1983: 849). The drafters left this question open. The unspecified metaphysical capacity might be construed positively because it allows for different cultures to participate in the search concerning the distinctive aspect of our nature, or capacities, accounting for our moral specialness. The search for the capacity that accounts for our moral specialness or human dignity animates this book in its quest to offer a plausible account of moral status from an African perspective. The point, however, of this specific discussion is that it is the concept of moral status, a capacity-based approach, that grounds the entire edifice of human rights. If human dignity and human rights are to be democratic, that must depend on a feature that is equalizing. A capacity is an equalizing property, whereas performance is not. It is for this reason that the idea of human dignity that we have merely because we are human is powerful and relevant in the human rights discourse. It is this powerful intuition behind the idea of moral status that we believe renders the capacity-based approach to value to be of utmost importance, which the agent-centred approach does not seem to have resources to accommodate.

In this section, I outlined some of the moral-theoretical advantages of the capacity-based approach to value theory, which I believe warrants us taking it seriously in African philosophy. The idea of moral status offers us a powerful approach to conceptualize the inviolability of certain candidates (the young, marginal cases, and animals) based on certain capacities or standing in a particular relationship to these capacities in their group. The agent-centred approach does not seem to have a satisfactory approach to offer moral-political protections to these beings. The idea of moral status explains the sources of our obligations in relation to the kinds of things we are, and failure to recognize the kinds of things we are may lead to the agent making our lives worse off. The agent-centred approach either offers an indirect defence of our duties towards them or appeals to the unrefined and unclarified idea of "it is a reasonable thing to do". In the idea of moral status, our duties track the moral patient herself, which status she enjoys because she possesses certain features. It is not entirely clear how the agent-centred approach can account for the idea of a moral patient, given that capacities of those who cannot use them are morally neutral. Remember that the value of capacities arises only in the context of their positive use to pursue personhood or moral dignity.

Second, we noted that the idea of moral status offers a robust approach to account for the equality of human beings by appeal to certain capacities that explain our status of dignity, whereas the agent-centred approach appeals to a variant property of performance/merit that fails to secure the concept of equality. Finally, we considered the importance of the capacity-based approach to human dignity in the modern political culture of human rights as captured in the UDHR. Human beings have intrinsic value, or moral status, because they possess certain capacities, and by virtue of being so valuable, they require us to live in decent conditions.

Conclusion

There might be good reasons to be suspicious of capacity-based approaches to value. This approach to value theory has been home to dangerous political regimes and experiments in human history, and it is still open to very serious abuses. The political danger can present itself in at least two ways. On the one hand, a shared property of our nature (such as rationality) may be denied to one group by another, thereby dehumanizing it and consequently stripping it of its moral status and the obligations that come with it. The colonial project seems to have operated on denying that Black people had the (rational) property that all human beings have, and from this denial, the looting, the enslavement, and genocide ensued against Black people (Ramose, 2002). On the other hand, an arbitrary feature that has no connection at all with morality may be posited as the basis for moral status, and all those who lack this insignificant capacity or property will be denied moral status, and subsequently, they are exposed to all kinds of vulnerabilities, horrors, and suffering in the world. The perfect example here is that of the property of skin pigmentation (race). The moral flaw of racism is a function of it assigning moral and political status based on an arbitrary and insignificant biological feature.

We are highlighting the ways that capacity-based approaches can go wrong because we share a similar worry with scholars of African thought that doubt its relevance and potency in ethics and politics (particularly in cases where we select an obviously problematic capacity or feature of human nature). We, however, do believe that it is rather reckless to give up on the intuition that there is something significant or special by human beings, which we explain in terms of significant aspects of our nature. Aristotle's distinction between the accidental and essential features of our nature captures the normative components of our nature that connect us directly to morality. The nutritive and reproductive aspects of our existence are natural components of our existence that we share with much of the animal community. Rational nature captures the normative aspects of our nature that connect us to morality. It is the insight that there is something morally special about human beings, which we explain in terms of capacities that seem directly connected with morality, that renders the approach inherent in the idea of moral status attractive.

The next chapter articulates an African conception of moral status.

Note

1 The reader might wonder how I may justify the view that the concept of moral status is hierarchical on the one hand and, on the other, it is a threshold and range concept in light of African thought. It is interesting to note that African metaphysical thought that scholars that work on the idea of human dignity invoke is hierarchical. It is hierarchical in that it places things in the cosmos on the different strata in the hierarchy. Cutting off the suprasensible part of the hierarchy, human beings occupy the highest position, followed by animals, inanimate things, and non-inanimate things at the bottom of the hierarchy (Magesa, 1997; Shutte, 2001). Scholars often associate the

highest stratum associated with human beings in the hierarchy with human dignity (Metz, 2012; Molefe, 2022). In this light, the picture that is usually associated with moral status and gradations relative to different stratum is inherent in African metaphysical and axiological thought.

References

Behrens, K. (2013). Two 'Normative' Conceptions of Personhood. *Quest* 25: 103–119.
Brennan, A., & Lo, Y. (2007). Two Conceptions of Human Dignity: Honour and Self-Determination. In J. Malpas & N. Lickiss (Eds.), *Perspectives on Human Dignity: A Conversation*. Dordrecht, The Netherlands: Springer, 39–47.
Darwall, S. (1977). Two Kinds of Respect. *Ethics* 80: 36–49.
DeGrazia, D. (2008). Moral Status as a Matter of Degree. *The Southern Journal of Philosophy* 48: 181–198.
DeGrazia, D. (2013). Equal Consideration and Unequal Moral Status. *The Southern Journal of Philosophy* 31: 17–31.
Donnelly, J. (2009). *Human Dignity and Human Rights*. Denver: Josef Korbel School of International Studies.
Freeman, M. (2015). Are there Collective Human Rights. *Political Studies* 43: 25–40.
Griffin, J. (2008). *On Human Rights*. Oxford: Oxford University Press.
Gyekye, K. (1992). Person and Community in African Thought. *Person and Community: Ghanaian Philosophical Studies*, 1. Washington DC: Council for Research in Values and Philosophy, 101–122.
Gyekye, K. (2010). African Ethics. In E. N. Zalta (Ed.), *The Stanford Encyclopedia of Philosophy*. http://plato.stanford.edu/archives/fall2011/entries/african-ethics (accessed 16 January 2013).
Habermas, J. (2010). The Concept of Human Dignity and the Realistic Utopia of Human Rights. *Metaphilosophy* 41: 464–480.
Hursthouse, R. (2013). Moral status. In *International encyclopedia of ethics*. Hoboken, NJ: John Wiley & Sons.
Ikuenobe, P. (2015). Relational Autonomy, Personhood, and African Traditions. *Philosophy East and West* 65: 1005–1029.
Ikuenobe, P. (2016). Good and Beautiful: A Moral-Aesthetic View of Personhood in African Communal Traditions. *Essays in Philosophy* 17: 124–163.
Ikuenobe, P. (2017). The Communal Basis for Moral Dignity: An African Perspective. *Philosophical Papers* 45: 437–469.
Ikuenobe, P. (2018). Human Rights, Personhood, Dignity, and African Communalism. *Journal of Human Rights* 17: 89–604.
Jaworska, A., & Tannenbaum, J. (2019). The Grounds of Moral Status. In E. Zalta (Ed.), *The Stanford Encyclopedia of Philosophy*. https://plato.stanford.edu/entries/groundsmoral-status/ (accessed 14 February 2023).
Kittay, E. (2005). Equality, Dignity and Disability. In M. A. Waldron & F. Lyons (Eds.), *Perspectives on Equality: The Second Seamus Heaney Lectures*. Dublin: Liffey, 95–122.
Korsgaard, C. (1983). Two Distinctions in Goodness. *Philosophical Review* 92: 69–195.
Korsgaard, C. (1996). *The Sources of Normativity*. Cambridge: Cambridge University Press.
Magesa, L. (1997). *African Religion: The Moral Traditions of Abundant Life*. New York: Orbis Books.
May, T. (2014). "Moral Individualism, Moral Relationalism and Obligations to Nonhuman Animals." *Journal of Applied Ethics* 31: 155–168.

Menkiti, I. (1984). Person and Community in African Traditional Thought. In R. A. Wright (Ed.), *African Philosophy: An Introduction*. Lanham: University Press of America, 171–181.

Menkiti, I. (2004). On the Normative Conception of a Person. In K. Wiredu (Ed.), *Companion to African Philosophy*. Oxford: Blackwell Publishing, 324–331.

Metz, T. (2012). An African theory of moral status: a relational alternative to individualism and holism. *Ethical Theory Moral Practice: International Forum* 14: 387–402.

Metz, T. (2021). *A Relational Moral Theory: African Ethics in and Beyond the Continent*. Oxford: Oxford University Press.

Miller, S. (2017). Reconsidering Dignity Relationally. *Ethics and Social Welfare* 11: 108–121.

Molefe, M. (2019). *An African Philosophy of Personhood, Morality and Politics*. New York: Palgrave Macmillan.

Molefe, M. (2020). *African Personhood and Applied Ethics*. Grahamstown: NISC [Pty]Ltd.

Molefe, M. (2022). *Human Dignity in African Philosophy: A Very Short Introduction*. Cham: Springer.

Nussbaum, M. (2011). *Creating Capabilities: The Human Development Approach*. Cambridge, MA: The Belknap Press of Harvard University Press.

Ramose, M. (2003). The Ethics of Ubuntu. In P. Coetzee and A. Roux, (Eds.), *The African Philosophy Reader* 324–331. New York, NY: Routledge.

Regan, T. (1985). The Case for Animal Rights. In P. Singer (Ed.), *In Defense of Animals*. Oxford: Basil Blackwell, 13–26.

Rosen, M. (2012). *Dignity: Its History and Meaning*. Cambridge, MA: Harvard University Press.

Schachter, O. (1983). The Normative Character of Personhood. *The American Journal of International Law* 77: 848–854.

Schroeder, D., & Bani-Sadr, A. (2017). *Dignity in the 21st Century Middle East and West*. New York: Springer Open.

Sen, A. (2001). *Development as Freedom*. New York: Alfred Knopf.

Shutte, A. (2001). *Ubuntu: An Ethic for a New South Africa*. Pietermaritzburg: Cluster Publications.

Singer, P. (2009). Speciesism and Moral Status. *Metaphilosophy* 40: 567–581.

Sulmasy, D. (2008). Dignity and bioethics: history, theory, and selected applications. In: The President's Council on bioethics, human dignity and bioethics: essays Commissioned by the President's Council. *President's Council on Bioethics*, Washington, DC, pp. 469–501.

Toscano, M. (2011). Human Dignity as High Moral Status. *The Ethics Forum* 6: 4–25.

UN. (1948). *Universal Declaration of Human Rights*. United Nations. http://www.un.org/en/universal-declaration-human-rights/.

Waldron, J. (2009). *Dignity, Rank, Rights*. The Tanner Lectures on Human Values. Delivered at the University of California, Berkeley.

Warren, A. (1997). *Moral Status: Obligations to Persons and Other Living Things*. Oxford: Clarendon Press.

Wasserman, D., Asch, D., Blustein, A., & Putnam, D. (2017). Cognitive Disability and Moral Status. In E. N. Zalta (Ed.), *The Stanford Encyclopedia of Philosophy*. https://plato.stanford.edu/archives/fall2017/entries/cognitive-disability/.

Wiredu, K. (2004). Introduction: African Philosophy in our Time. In K. Wiredu, (Ed.), *Companion to African Philosophy*, 1–27. Oxford: Blackwell Publishing.

Wood, A. (1998). Kant on Duties Regarding Non-Rational Nature. *Proceedings of the Aristotelian Society Supplement* 72: 189–210.

3 Ubuntu Ethics, *ubuntu*, and Moral Status

Introduction

The chapter articulates an Ubuntu-based account of moral status. Ubuntu ethics comprises three components, namely, (1) the final good, (2) moral status, and (3) moral relationalism. The book focuses on moral status and its application to the question of death. To articulate an Ubuntu-based account of moral status, we will limit our focus to the two components of Ubuntu ethics: (1) the final good and (2) moral status. Ubuntu ethics prescribes *ubuntu*, or virtue, as the final good, which requires moral agents to acquire *ubuntu*. We focus on (1) and (2) because we derive our theory of moral status (2) from the final good (1), that is, an account of moral status will be a function of whatever we will specify as the content of the final good. We will interpret Ubuntu ethics to account for *ubuntu*, the final good, in terms of empathy. If we derive our theory of moral status from the final good of *ubuntu*, which we will understand in terms of empathy, then it will follow that Ubuntu ethics accounts for moral status in terms of the human capacity for empathy.

To clarify the logical structure of our argument, note two crucial considerations that relate to our strategy to articulate an Ubuntu-based account of moral status. First, our strategy involves inferring (or presuming) a conception of moral status from a conception of the final good. We justify this strategy by the "ought implies can" principle. The "ought implies can" principle indicates "that moral demands cannot be incompatible with our human potentials and capacities. Our moral theories must be practicable" (Sherman, 1998: 84). Moral theories prescribe standards of acceptable conduct or excellence. Moral agents are expected to live up to the demands of morality. We interpret the "ought implies can" principle to embody the insight that the prescriptions of morality make sense when we understand them to presume a metaphysical basis (potentials and capacities), which renders demands of morality practicable. That is, if Ubuntu ethics prescribes the acquisition of *ubuntu* (or virtue), then it makes sense to presume or even infer that this moral expectation must be informed by an (unspecified) commitment that human beings possess certain metaphysical potentials and capacities to pursue and acquire it (*ubuntu*).

DOI: 10.4324/9781032658490-4

Hence, Ubuntu ethics prescribes the acquisition of *ubuntu* (or virtue) because moral agents have the metaphysical capacity for it. The logical structure of our argument is that we can infer an account of moral status (the metaphysical capacities grounding what the possibility of what the moral theory prescribes) from what a moral theory prescribes. Hence, we account for moral status in terms of the metaphysical capacity for *ubuntu* (or empathy).

Notice that we distinguish between the two components of the "ought implies can" principle: the "*can*" part and the "*ought*" part. In our view, the "ought" part refers to the final good (the obligations imposed by morality), and the "can" part refers to the intrinsic good or moral status (the metaphysical aspects of our nature that render us able to fulfil the demands of morality). Christine Korsgaard (1983) brilliantly distinguishes the final good from the intrinsic good. The final good is contrasted against an instrumental one. We value an instrumental good in relation to its usefulness or its outcomes. Money is a good example of an instrumental good; we value it for its usefulness in the market to facilitate transactions. A final good, on the other hand, is to be valued in itself and/or for its own sake. Things like truth, in many occasions, count among those that we should value for their own sakes. Most people, for example, would rather know the truth about their cheating partner no matter its consequences than to live in deception – there is something worthwhile about living in truth than living in deception. An intrinsic good, on the other hand, refers to the source or location of goodness specifically that it is internal of the object under consideration. For example, when we claim that beauty is intrinsically good, we are claiming that the location of its goodness is in beauty itself. The final good specifies the goal of morality that we ought to value and pursue for its own sake, and the intrinsic good specifies the source or location of the goodness of the object under consideration.

Our interpretation of Ubuntu ethics imposes a connection between the final good (the ought part) and the intrinsic good (the can part), where we presume the former presupposes the latter. The logic of our argument is that the salient belief in Ubuntu thinking that we ought to acquire *ubuntu*, the final good, presumes, or we can infer from it, that we should have the metaphysical capacity to achieving it, intrinsic goodness. Depending on how we account for the final good of *ubuntu*, we shall account for moral status as the underlying metaphysical capacity for it (*ubuntu*) (the final good). Our strategy involves a philosophical exposition of *ubuntu* (the final good), which we will understand in terms of cultivated empathy, and we will account for moral status, given our rendition of the "ought implies can" principle, as the capacity for empathy. In our view, the "ought implies can" principle marries the final good (*ubuntu* construed in terms of cultivated empathy) and the moral status (the capacity for empathy), and we will account for the latter simply in terms of the capacity for the former.

Second, scholars in the literature on African ethics tend to account for *ubuntu* as the final good in terms of being *humane*. To have *ubuntu* is generally understood to denote being humane, and scholars usually associate being humane with a variety of pro-social attitudes and behaviours such as compassion, kindness, friendliness, and so on (Ramose, 1999; Tutu, 1999; Munyaka & Motlhabi, 2009; Murove, 2014; Etieyibo, 2017). To attempt precision on the nature of *ubuntu* as the final good, we will attempt to give content to what it means to be humane by making several illuminating revisions. We will first attempt to interpret *ubuntu* (or being humane) in terms of altruism. Ultimately, we will account for *ubuntu* in terms of empathy that triggers altruism. Thus, to have *ubuntu* is the same as to have empathy. The final good of *ubuntu* is equivalent to developed empathy. We will further conceive of empathy to be intrinsically associated with altruism. Hence, we will argue that Ubuntu thinking accounts for moral status in terms of our capacity for empathy.

To articulate an Ubuntu-based account of moral status, which we will derive from the final good of *ubuntu*, we structure the chapter as follows. The first section aims to explicate a plausible account of the final good, *ubuntu*. Our search for a plausible interpretation of *ubuntu*, the final good, will proceed as follows: (a) the general account of the final good, where we will explain *ubuntu* in terms of being humane (which is a common view in the literature); (b) we will proceed to give content to the final good of *ubuntu* (or being humane) by interpreting it in terms of altruism; and (c) we will finally amend our understanding of *ubuntu* to explain it in terms of empathy. (Our interpretation of Ubuntu thinking in terms of empathy will take the empathy–altruism hypothesis seriously, where empathy tends to trigger altruistic motivations and actions.) In the final section, drawing from the "ought implies can" principle, we will posit that Ubuntu ethics accounts for moral status in terms of the capacity for empathy.

The Final Good (General Account)

This chapter, and the rest of the book, operates based on the distinction between Ubuntu and *ubuntu*; the former refers to the whole system of philosophy (with its own metaphysics, epistemology, and axiology) associated with African peoples, what we might describe as African philosophy. The latter refers to what Ubuntu axiology prescribes as the final good, the good, which the agent ought to pursue and acquire. The former is a property of a cultural group, Africans or African cultures, and the latter is a property of a person who ought to acquire *ubuntu*. Ubuntu ethics emerges in generally nonliterate contexts, where literacy was not the dominant mode of cultural expression. African people developed sophisticated oral techniques to preserve and convey deep moral principles (see Shutte, 2001). It is therefore not surprising that Ubuntu ethics is generally captured via the saying *Umuntu ngumuntu ngabantu*, or in English, "a person is a person through other persons". The saying embodies the core meaning of African moral thought. Notice the repetition of the word *umuntu*/person – the saying repeats the word three times.

Ubuntu Ethics, Ubuntu, and Moral Status 43

We suggest that to make a headway in understanding Ubuntu ethics, we need to pay special attention to the first two concepts of a person in the proverb – "a person is a person" – because the first instance of the word corresponds to the concept of moral status (or human dignity), which we interpret to refer to the ontological concept of a person. The second instance refers to the final good, *ubuntu*, or becoming a person, which we understand as the normative concept of a person. Remember, we will derive the former, a conception of moral status, from the latter, the normative concept of a person.[1]

The phrase "a person is a person" draws a distinction between the fact of being human and the moral goal of becoming a person. Consider the comment by Ramose (2003: 413):

> [T]he concept of a person in African thought takes the fact of being a human being for granted. It is assumed that one cannot discuss the concept of personhood without in the first place admitting the "human existence" of the human being upon whom personhood is to be conferred.

Ramose draws a distinction between being human (what he calls *human existence*) and being a person (which personhood we confer onto a human being). (The distinction between a human and a person can also be expressed in terms of the distinction between ontological and normative concepts of a person.) The status of a person is conferred onto a human being. The former is an ontological given – it is prior to the latter – and the latter is conferred onto a person – s/he acquires it, relative to the quality of her conduct. Being human is necessary for a person, but it is not sufficient for it; the agent must cultivate or acquire it.

To further clarify the relation between the ontological and normative concepts of a person, we consider Ifeanyi Menkiti's explication of this relationship. Menkiti is probably the most influential scholar of African personhood. Menkiti (1984: 172) avers:

> It is not enough to have before us the biological organism, with whatever rudimentary psychological characteristics are seen as attaching to it. We must also conceive of this organism as going through a long process of social and ritual transformation until it attains the full complement of excellencies seen as truly definitive of man.

On Menkiti's view, a human being possesses certain ontological capacities, which he describes as *rudimentary psychological characteristics*. (Remember, for Menkiti, ontological capacities do not possess any intrinsic value.) The biological organism, a human being, Menkiti rightly observes, is necessary for personhood, but not sufficient for it. Menkiti informs us that we must think of the acquisition of personhood as a process. The moral agent must engage in a process of sociomoral transformation. The aim of the process involves transitioning from being a biological organism to truly becoming a person, that is, a human being exuding with virtue. Menkiti prefers the word *excellence* as definitive of the status of personhood. We understand the concept of "excellence" to refer to an agent with a virtuous character disposition (Gyekye, 2010). The more excellences the agent acquires, the more of a person she becomes, and *vice versa*. We can summarize Menkiti's understanding of personhood to amount to the view that it involves (or emerges because of) the process where what was initially merely a biological organism, a human being, engages in the process of the "ingathering of the excellences" so she may become a "bearer of norms", or one with a virtuous disposition (2004: 325–326).

In light of the aforementioned, we express the final good associated with Ubuntu ethics in terms of either acquiring *ubuntu* or becoming a person whose expressions are equivalent ways of associating the agent with excellence or virtue (see Ikuenobe, 2017). What is the content of *ubuntu* or the status of a person? First, scholars explain *ubuntu* as an innate or inner quality that captures the essence of our humanity and morality. Munyaka and Motlhabi (2009: 64) associate having *ubuntu* with the development of the "most important quality" of our human nature. They also describe it as a "positive quality" of our nature "that can fluctuate from the lowest to the highest level during one's lifetime" (ibid., 64; Mokgoro, 1998: 2). To have *ubuntu* or to become a person essentially involves the development of this inner quality of our nature. Second, scholars of African thought tend to interpret the positive inner quality of our nature, when properly cultivated, as being *humane*, and scholars tend to associate (being humane) with other-regarding attitudes and pro-social behaviours (Ramose, 1999).

For example, Felix Murove (2014: 37) informs us, "Ubuntu means humaneness – treating other people with kindness, compassion, respect and care. These virtues are usually referred to as the summation of *humaneness*". Edwin Etieyibo (2017: 141) speaks of *ubuntu*, which he understands in terms of being humane, "as roughly about human kindness". Desmond Tutu (1999: 31) makes sense of the humaneness associated with *ubuntu* in this fashion: "When we want to give high praise to someone we say, 'Yu, u nobuntu'; 'Hey, so-and-so has ubuntu.' Then, you are generous, you are hospitable, you are friendly and caring and compassionate. You share what you have". Nyasani (1989: 9) associates *ubuntu* with "virtues like patience, optimism, mutual sympathy and empathy". In their brilliant essay on Ubuntu ethics, Munyaka and Motlhabi (2009: 65) associate the cultivation of *ubuntu* "with a disposition which motivates, challenges . . . one . . . [to] act in humane ways towards others", and they further associate being humane with "mutuality" (65), "sympathy" (71), "kindness, compassion, caring, sharing, solidarity and sacrifice" (74), among others. Finally, consider Gyekye's description of features characteristic of becoming a person. Gyekye (1992: 116) associates becoming a person with "moral virtues that can be said to include generosity, kindness, compassion, benevolence, respect and concern for others; in fine, any action or behaviour that conduces to the promotion of the welfare of others". Note that Gyekye (1992: 110) construes becoming a person in terms of the display of other-regarding virtues (see Gyekye, 2010).

The preceding quotations justify the conclusion that to have *ubuntu* (or to become a person) is tantamount to being humane, which character disposition characteristically expresses itself through other-regarding attitudes and/or pro-social behaviour (or relational virtues). Relational virtues are the kinds of virtues that presuppose or require a relationship with another for their development and/or expression. Compassion, for example, at the very least, presupposes another person (could be a sentient being) as its object. Relational virtues have an essential other-regarding feature, where another human being is their target. When we say one has *ubuntu*, we are actually praising the agent for having acquired a humane disposition characterized by relational virtues that benefit others. The same goes for attributing personhood to some agent. Hence, Wiredu (2009: 15) informs us that "to be called a person is to be commended". Personhood and/or *ubuntu* are terms of moral recognition, praise, or even approbation which track the quality of the agent's character in relation to how she regards, relates, and treats other human beings with kindness and respect, among others.

To have *ubuntu* or to become a person involves the agent developing or cultivating the inner quality of our nature in the context of a positive relationship with others to be characterized as virtue or excellence, which character disposition of virtue we explain in terms of being humane. We observe that Ubuntu ethics belongs to the cluster of moral theories described as *self-realization* or *perfectionist* (Wall, 2012; Molefe, 2019). Self-realization or perfectionist theories of value tend to prescribe the development of certain features of our nature as *the* goal of morality. For example, Ngcoya (2015: 253) offers what we consider to be a self-realization interpretation of Ubuntu ethics when he opines, "[L]iving is ultimately the discovery and realization of –ntu (person) and this is only accomplished through other –ntu (person)". Metz (2007: 331), in his search for a plausible interpretation of Ubuntu ethics, makes the following observation: "This is probably the dominant interpretation of African ethics in the literature. Many thinkers take the maxim 'a person is a person through other persons' to be a call for an agent to develop her personhood". He describes an approach to morality that requires the agent to become a person as a "self-realization" theory of value because it involves the agent perfecting or developing valuable aspects of her nature (ibid.). Behrens (2013: 111) is correct to make the following comment regarding Menkiti's associated personhood with the agent realizing her true moral destiny in this fashion:

> Menkiti's association of the term "excellencies" with personhood also implies that becoming a person is essentially related to developing virtue. Thus, the African conception of personhood could be thought of as

proposing a theory of ethics that brings to mind what Western philosophy calls "perfectionism": Persons should seek to develop a good or virtuous nature to become true or fully moral persons.

Ubuntu ethics embodies a perfectionist or a self-realization account of ethics, where the moral agent, possessing certain inner qualities, has a duty to cultivate them to embody *ubuntu* or for the agent to become a person. The perfection of our human nature involves developing or nurturing it to be characterized by virtue, where we can say she has *ubuntu* (or is humane).

To obtain a more accurate picture of African ethics, we need to clarify the association between *ubuntu* and relational virtues. Emphasis on relational virtues as a characteristic feature of *ubuntu* raises serious questions about the place of the individual or self-regarding duties in African ethics (Molefe, 2022). A plausible interpretation of Ubuntu ethics should accommodate both the self-regarding and the other-regarding components (Lenka-Bula, 2008). The reason for including the self-regarding component is not far to seek. A careful observer will notice that the inner quality that must be cultivated is the property of the individual. The cultivation of this property amounts to morally developing morally relevant metaphysical capacities of our nature. Hence, having *ubuntu* is a moral statement about the agent's chief moral task of self-development, or personal perfection. It follows that a proper interpretation of the acquisition of *ubuntu* must not lose sight of its essential agent-centred aspect, which we can rightly describe as having an essentially self-regarding activity involving the agent focusing on their personal moral development.[2]

The emphasis on relational virtues is important because it specifies two crucial considerations associated with the acquisition of *ubuntu*. First, it specifies the nature of the virtues associated with it that are other-oriented or relational, such as generosity and friendliness. Second, it specifies the context within which the agent can learn, practice, and exercise such relational virtues in social relationships or the community. It is the agent that pursues *ubuntu*, and it is only the agent that can acquire *ubuntu*, whose process involves the cultivation of raw qualities of her nature. It must be noted, however, that she can only do so in the context of positively relating with others, in which positive relations provide a context for learning and exercising relational virtues. The interpretation that accommodates the self- and other-regarding components of *ubuntu* finds support in the aphorism definitive of African moral thought: "I am because we are". The "I am" part refers to the agent that ought to cultivate a humane disposition, and the "we are" part indicates the social context that provides the resources and opportunities through which the agent can learn, develop, and exercise *ubuntu*. Hence, Munyaka and Motlhabi (2009: 70) appositely note, "It is in a human community that an individual is able to realize himself or herself as a person". The perfection of the agent's valuable nature, the acquisition of *ubuntu*, is inseparable from engaging in positive or other-regarding relationships, where one learns, develops, and acquires *ubuntu*.

On first approximation, Ubuntu ethics accounts for the final good of *ubuntu* in terms of being humane, which character disposition finds expression *via* relational virtues, that is, other-regarding virtues, such as kindness, compassion, generosity, and so on. In what follows, we aim to offer a more precise understanding of what is involved in being humane or having *ubuntu*, which we believe will contribute to Ubuntu thinking.[3]

The Final Good (*ubuntu* as Altruism)

Several scholars have proposed a variety of moral concepts or virtues to account for *ubuntu*, such as harmony, critical humanism, vitality, and friendliness (Molefe, 2019b). The literature has already indicated that these interpretations of Ubuntu ethics, in one way or another, are inadequate (Oyowe, 2013; Matolino & Kwindingwi, 2013; Molefe, 2017, 2019). Another prominent feature associated with the agent with *ubuntu* is the disposition to be sharing or of altruism (Wiredu, 1992; Tutu, 1999; Murove, 2014; Metz, 2007; Munyaka & Motlhabi, 2009; Gyekye, 2010). Altruism seems to be a promising candidate to explain what it means to have *ubuntu* (or being humane). On this suggestion, to have *ubuntu*, or to be humane, denotes being altruistic. Essentially, altruism has two elements: "Altruism is generally understood to be behaviour that benefits others [even] at a personal cost to the behaving individual" (Kerr, Godrey-Smith & Feldmann, 2004: 135). The first and essential element of altruism is the motivation and action that benefits others. The second element is that sometimes altruism may be at a personal cost of the agent in their quest to benefit another.

We believe that both features of altruism characterize what it means to have *ubuntu* or to be humane. Altruism is a promising candidate to account for being humane precisely because it seems compatible with a plethora of pro-social attitudes and behaviours associated with it. The agent that has *ubuntu*, or is humane, is one that is characteristically altruistic. This suggestion finds some support in the literature. Molema (1920: 110) indicates that altruism underlies the good of each individual and community in African moral thought. Gyekye (2010), in an encyclopaedic entry dedicated to African ethics, observes that "altruism is, thus, a fundamental moral value". Commenting on attempts to ground post-independence politics on African values, Dismas Masolo observes that post-independence leaders (such as Julius Nyerere and Kenneth Kaunda, among others) construed African socialism as "a secular set of humane values based on altruism as the basis of social unity and cooperation". Nyerere's *Ujamma* moral-political project of a post-independence society and economy operated based on sharing and altruism as an expression of being humane, or *ubuntu*. Masolo's (2004: 494, emphasis mine) elucidation of Afro-communitarian ethics accounts for it in terms of what he calls practical altruism in this fashion:

> In its moral definition, communitarianism describes the belief in the principle of practical altruism as an important social virtue. It recognizes and

encourages *sharing with others* as an important characteristic of human life. Like everywhere else in human societies, *African communitarianism is a principle for guiding the practice of everyday life in ways that aim at creating a humane world* in which, to quote from Wiredu, "individuals will have the chance of realizing their interests, conceived as being intrinsically bound up with the interests of others in society."

In light of the common tendency by scholars of African thought to define *ubuntu* in terms of being humane, Masolo connects the practice of altruism with being humane or creating a humane world. Masolo explains being humane or creating a humane world in terms of sharing with others, or what he describes as *practical altruism*. Hence, we can construe the communitarian value of *ubuntu*, the final good, in terms of practical altruism, that is, the essence of *ubuntu* practical altruism. To have *ubuntu*, on this rendition, is just to be motivated by altruistic concerns. We note three things about *ubuntu* interpreted in terms of practical altruism. First, Masolo describes it as "*practical* altruism" to capture the idea that it ought to be a principle that characterizes agents' conduct on a daily basis. Second, Masolo describes altruism as a "*social* virtue". To describe altruism as a *social* virtue echoes the elevated place that a communitarian ethic places on relational virtues, which according to Gyekye (2010, emphasis mine) "mandates a morality that clearly is weighted on duty to others and to the community". Practical altruism places an emphasis on other-regarding duties.

The final aspect associated with *ubuntu* construes it in terms of altruism and involves specifying the essential purpose of the benefit it seeks to impart towards its objects. Often, scholars narrowly limit it to promoting human well-being. Many scholars of African thought tend to wrongly reduce the purpose, the final good, of Afro-communitarianism to securing human well-being (Wiredu, 1992; Gyekye, 2004; Masolo, 2010; Okeja, 2013). In our view, human well-being is important and does have its place in a robust ethical system, but it is not the final good.[4] The essence of the benefit to another associated with altruism involves contributing to creating a humane world, what Biko (2004: 64) refers to as the "human face", so that others can be empowered to be humane or live under conditions that conduces towards being humane.

Altruism does add something positive to our understanding of *ubuntu*. A humane disposition is characteristically altruistic. We believe, however, that this needs further clarification. The basic motivation underlying altruism is another person since it aims to alleviate their need or promote their good. The reader must keep in mind, however, that we had already noted that *ubuntu* has an essential self-regarding component, which any robust moral system ought to have (Molefe, 2021). The challenge before us involves clarifying the potential tension between the essentially self-regarding element of *ubuntu* and our characterization of it in terms of altruism. The goal of realizing one's true nature, to have *ubuntu*, seems to pull in a different direction than the entirely other-regarding element characteristic of altruism.

To diffuse the seeming tension between the self-regarding element of *ubuntu* and altruism, we begin by noting that the problem in the literature on altruism is that it tends to construe it in terms of either/or, where the interests of the agent are imagined as always opposed to those of another person. We propose a moderate version of altruism. In a very interesting essay, Elliot Sober (1991) differentiates among extreme altruism (the agent is strictly concerned with promoting the good of the other), moderate altruism (the good of the self and another intersect), extreme egoism (the self is concerned strictly with her own good), and moderate egoism (the good of the self and the other intersect). We reject both extreme altruism and extreme egoism since they fail to accommodate the good of both the agent and another. Remember that the proverb "a person is a person through other persons" underscores the view that the good of the agent cannot or ought never to be separated from the good of another. The pressing question before us then involves us justifying the interpretation of Ubuntu ethics as moderately altruistic as opposed to it being moderately egoistic.

Space does not permit an exhaustive treatment of this problem. It suffices that we offer preliminary reasons that suggest that African ethics embody moderate altruism. In the debate concerning the plausibility of the self-realization interpretation of Ubuntu ethics, Metz (2007: 332) objects to it because it fails to give a good reason for altruism. He expresses the objection as follows:

> I now question the theory's ability to provide an attractive explanation of them. If I ask why I should help others, for example, this theory says that the basic justificatory reason to do so . . . is that it will help me by making me more of . . . a better person. However, a better fundamental explanation of why I ought to help others appeals not to the fact that it would be good for me, or at least not merely to this fact, but to the fact that it would (likely) be good for them, an explanation that a self-realization ethic by definition cannot invoke.

The wrong assumption underlying this objection towards the self-realization interpretation of Ubuntu ethics is that it assumes a strict dichotomy between the good of the altruistic agent and the object altruism. David Lutz (2009: 316), responding to Metz's strict dichotomy between the agent's good and another's, rightly identifies the source of this dichotomy when he opines that "[m]odern European moral philosophy assumes what Sidgwick . . . calls 'the dualism of practical reason' and Lewis . . . calls 'the philosophy of hell': the idea that one person's good is separate from another's". African ethics should be correctly construed to operate; in fact, it insists on the moral logic, where agents understand their interests (or even good) "as being intrinsically bound up with the interests of others in society" (Masolo, 2004: 498). Stated in different terms, Shutte (2001: 31) opines, "I only become fully human (attain *ubuntu*) to the extent that I am included in relationships with others".

Hence, we note that Ubuntu thinking insists on a moral perspective that seeks to secure the good of all, all things being equal. The good of acquiring *ubuntu*, which is a common good we can only attain in robust interpersonal relationships with others, where we positively support and help others, serves simultaneously as opportunities for self-empowerment by perfecting one's dispositions towards being more humane. Hence, we can rightly note that the kind of altruism associated with *ubuntu*, as the final good, is a moderate kind of altruism in that it values the good of the self as much as it values the good of another, since it considers them to be conjoined in a dynamic reciprocal relationship of exchange and empowerment. One opportunity to help another is a seed to add to my moral character, to grow and perfect it. The agent with *ubuntu* ought to be preoccupied with herself as much as she should be preoccupied with the other because she understands that "[she] cannot separate [her] humanity from the humanity of those around [her]" (Luthans et al., 2004: 515). Hence, we observe that a more accurate account of having *ubuntu* or being humane is a function of being moderately altruistic, all things being equal, the good of all intersects.

Second, the crucial difference between moderate altruism and moderate egoism, which informs why we rule out the latter, lies in that the former cannot, in principle, do an entirely other-regarding act where only the good of another is at stake even at the possible abridgement of one's own good. The essence of altruism is the focus on the good of another. You forgo the good of another as the goal or focus of the agent's actions; one can no longer meaningfully talk of altruism. In moderate egoism, the agent's self-interest, in a trade-off situation, ought to take priority over another. You remove self-interest as the focus and target of the agent's actions; we have lost the essence of egoism. On a prima facie basis, we posit that a plausible account of *ubuntu* ought to be able, in certain circumstances, to set aside one's good for the sake of purely promoting another's good. The paradigm example of this intuition or manifestation of *ubuntu* is captured by the act of self-sacrifice (Motlhabi & Munyaka, 2009). By "sacrifice" here we mean surrendering one's life for the sake of another's good. Think of the examples of struggle of heroes that fought for independence and freedom in African countries. The act of political martyrdom, as we see in Stephen Bantu Biko or Solomon Kalushi Mahlangu, among many others across the continent and the world, can be understood as instantiations of *ubuntu*, where the agent places the interest of the community over even their own personal existence.

We support moderate altruism over moderate egoism because the latter can never accommodate self-sacrifice as an instance of *ubuntu*, which we believe is a feature of a robust interpretation of Ubuntu ethics. The act of self-sacrifice is characteristically unselfish. Remember, according to Shutte, to have *ubuntu* refers to a process of personal (moral) growth that the agent achieves by increasingly entering the community, a process of personal transformation and development that should be devoid of selfishness. One way to think of selfishness is when one pursues personal growth at the expense of others or the community. Or pursues only for their own benefit. To clarify the point about selfishness, consider this case: The agent requires a kidney, and she can get it by killing (murder) a healthy person. The agent will survive and continue her self-interest of pursuing personhood in the long run by committing this heinous act of murder. Metz (2007) criticizes this crude version of moderate egoism, which should not be wrongly associated with the self-realization interpretation of Ubuntu ethics. We also reject it for three reasons. A moderate egoist (a) is prone to fall into selfishness (in that she arbitrarily values her own existence over that of another), (b) fails to respect the dignity of another human being by using her merely as a means for her own survival and health, and (3) is anti-community in that she pursues her interests in ways that do not recognize "through other persons" as a crucial means through which to pursue the good. One slips into the zone of selfishness when she fails to recognize and act cognizant to the fact that "[her] humanity is caught up, is inextricably bound up in [others']" (Tutu, 1999: 31).

Here we have accounted for having *ubuntu*, personhood, and being humane in terms of moderate altruism, where the goal of personal moral growth is conjoined with the goal of contributing to the moral growth of others. We believe it will be more accurate to account for *ubuntu* in terms of empathy than merely as altruism. We make this move because we take seriously the psycho-moral thesis that posits a correlation between empathy and altruism. We motivate and develop this line of reasoning in the next section. We do not displace moderate altruism as part of *ubuntu*; we clarify its role in terms of the underlying virtue of empathy.

Next, we propose empathy as the essence of *ubuntu*, in which empathy tends to trigger altruism.

The Final Good: *ubuntu* as Empathy

Here, we make one final amendment to the common interpretation of *ubuntu* as being humane. First, we note that having *ubuntu* denotes being altruistic. We propose that a more accurate interpretation of Ubuntu ethics ought to distinguish the essence of *ubuntu* from its manifestation in attitudes and actions. We propose this distinction because we hold the intuition that something deeper grounds altruism, and it is this deep thing that captures the essence of *ubuntu*. We propose that we should properly understand the achievement of *ubuntu* with developed empathy, that is, to have *ubuntu* is to make reference or denotes empathy as the defining essence of African moral thought, and developed empathy tends to correlate with altruism. Roughly, we understand "empathy as a way of understanding others that is emotionally responsive and supportive, and in an overall way, altruistic" (Sherman, 1998: 86). A close reading of the literature on Ubuntu thinking imagines an agent that has a deep understanding of another, which understanding grounds emotional responsiveness, which informs altruism (or caring), on our part, moderate altruism. Our view is that to have *ubuntu* means having developed empathy, and empathy induces care.

Two major reasons motivate the move to interpret *ubuntu* in terms of empathy and its link to altruism. First, our friends in the Western tradition of philosophy and psychology had long anticipated the link between empathy and altruism. Moral sentimentalism, as championed by scholars such as Hutcheson, David Hume, and Adam Smith, among others, ground morality on sentiments, which they tend to explain in terms of sympathy or empathy. Commenting on these scholars, Sherman (1998: 85) remarks, "Perhaps the most direct application of empathy in moral theory rests on some claim that it is correlated with altruistic motivation. This is an undercurrent in Hume's and Smith's writings, although it awaits twentieth-century psychology laboratory for its full exploration". Sherman could be construed to be making two crucial points. First, she notes that empathy, or sentiment, is the basis of morality. Second, she notes that sentimentalists had already anticipated or implied the positive relation between empathy and altruism.

More recently, Michael Slote defends a moral system, a revival of moral sentimentalism, which posits empathy as the sole foundation for morality (see 2007, 2010). Slote draws his account of ethics from eighteenth-century sentimentalists and modern psychology experiments, particularly the empathy–altruism hypothesis, to account for our moral obligations and the meta-ethical project of explaining the moral language of right and wrong in terms of empathy (Slote, 2007). In relation to the empathy–altruism hypothesis, Slote (2010: 6) observes:

> There is a vast literature on empathy and its role in altruism. So although this is anticipated by Hume, we now have a vast social-developmental literature in which the role of empathy as grounding and supporting and as necessary to altruism is much discussed.

Slote's approach to morality departs from the point of view that empathy is foundational in meta-ethics and normative ethics. He further observes that the empathy–altruism hypothesis is "by and large . . . fairly well is accepted in the social-psychological literature" (ibid.). We take seriously the view that morality revolves around sentiments (or empathy), because the intuition "that concern for others [altruism] is powered by and depends upon developed empathy" is present in African thought, but it is generally underexplored and developed (ibid.).

The second reason is that the literature on African ethics resonates with the moral intuition and moral theories that posit empathy as foundational in morality and that endorse the psycho-moral hypothesis that posits empathy as the basis for our altruistic motivations and actions. Notice that Wiredu's (1992) ethical theory reads much like an African version of moral sentimentalism. He describes his normative theory in terms of sympathetic/empathetic impartiality (he uses *sympathy* and *empathy* interchangeably). Wiredu (1996: 78) unequivocally states that empathy is "the root of all virtue". Kai Horsthemke (2015: 56) interprets the analogy of a root in Wiredu's articulation of African ethics to amount to the claim that empathy is the "very foundation of morality". We interpret the analogy of a root to suggest that empathy is the generative basis for all other virtues, that is, empathy is a root, and all other virtues are its fruits. Without the root, the stem, branches, leaves, and fruits cannot emerge. The root holds the tree and all its parts and their functions together. In this sense, we can interpret Wiredu to use the analogy of a root in relation empathy to be positing empathy as foundational in African ethics. Moreover, all other virtues, or pro-social behaviours associated with *ubuntu* (construed as empathy), emerge from it and because of it as instantiation of the altruism associated with it (empathy).

This underexplored interpretation of Ubuntu ethics in terms of empathy can also be associated with Shutte's interpretation of *ubuntu*, the final good. Shutte (2009: 98) observes, "The range of moral virtues that make up *ubuntu* is very wide". This claim that associates *ubuntu* with a wide range of pro-social attitudes and virtues does not come as a surprise. It is what he says next that we find most interesting. Shutte proceeds to observe that sympathy or empathy is among the most fundamental virtues in Ubuntu ethics. After observing the primacy of sympathy or empathy in Ubuntu ethics, Shutte further posits that from it (empathy) "grow other virtues such as loyalty, courtesy, tolerance, patience, generosity, hospitality and readiness to cooperate". We interpret Shutte to have anticipated a sentimentalist interpretation of Ubuntu ethics, where the sentiment of empathy is the defining feature, a fundamental virtue, and from it springs a wide range of pro-social attitudes and behaviours.

We read both Wiredu and Shutte to be presenting a picture of Ubuntu ethics where empathy is the root (foundation) of morality, which (empathy) induces towards other-regarding and pro-social virtues as its fruits. Hence, it strikes us as plausible to interpret Shutte to have anticipated the empathy–altruism hypothesis in his account of Ubuntu ethics, where empathy is a foundational value or virtue from which springs pro-social attitudes and behaviours (altruism). Hence, we note that the pursuit of *ubuntu* (or being humane) – remember, *ubuntu* is the final good – literally means, or we argue that it should be interpreted to refer to, the sociomoral process cultivating or developing empathy. To be humane denotes that one has a cultivated or developed empathy, which (empathy) involves the psychological ability to understand another from their internal/emotional standpoint (epistemic dimension of empathy) and to connect with them (relational component of empathy), which knowledge and connection (empathy) with another tends to be accompanied by concern or care (altruism) for another.

In summary, Ubuntu ethics prescribes the acquisition of *ubuntu* (or being humane) as the final good. Our purpose in this section involved offering a precise account of the content of *ubuntu* (the final) as a moral term. We began our search for a plausible characterization of *ubuntu* by noting the association between acquiring *ubuntu* and being humane, and being humane is usually associated with pro-social attitudes and conduct. Next, we illuminated being humane in terms of altruism, since due its relational orientation it best explains the pro-social attitudes and conduct associated with being humane (or having *ubuntu*). Given the association that philosophers (in the West and Africa) and psychologists posit between empathy and altruism, where the former is foundational and triggers the latter, we interpreted the acquisition of *ubuntu* with the cultivation of empathy. We have roughly characterized empathy as the ability to identify and connect with others, which recognizes, affirms, and responds to the human condition altruistically, or caringly. Thus, the saying "a person is a person through other persons" calls our attention to a moral perspective based on empathy to relate, treat, and respond to the human condition caringly.

We now turn to an Ubuntu-based account of moral status.

Ubuntu Ethics and Moral Status

We interpret the "ought implies can" principle in such a way that we can infer, or presume, that it embodies a conception of moral status as the basis for the general belief in Ubuntu thinking that human beings can acquire *ubuntu*, or empathy. If Ubuntu thinking prescribes the cultivation of empathy, or *ubuntu*, as the final good, then we should have the metaphysical material that grounds and justifies the moral demands or expectations. Insistence that human beings must fulfil their obligations to acquire empathy necessarily implicates us in the belief that human beings do have the metaphysical capacity for empathy. We note that when scholars associate the possibility for the acquisition of *ubuntu* with the *inner quality* or *positive quality* of our nature that can either grow or deteriorate, we can interpret this talk of inner or positive quality to be a reference to the raw metaphysical for empathy. The acquisition of *ubuntu* is a function of the development of the raw capacities or qualities of our nature, which when cultivated amounts to *ubuntu* or developed empathy.

This way of interpreting Ubuntu ethics, where we distinguish the capacity for *ubuntu* (or empathy) and the actual cultivation and exercise of *ubuntu* (or empathy), does find support in the literature in African philosophy. Note Gyekye's (1997: 55) comment on African ethics:

> There are at least two senses in which an agent may be said to be moral: an agent may be said to be moral in the sense that he has the moral sense or capacity to distinguish between the good and evil, but he may also be said to be moral in the sense that he does that which is good and that his actions conform to the existing moral values or rules.

Gyekye distinguishes between two distinct senses of morality. The first sense of morality is action- or agent-centred in that it involves the agent performing some action, becoming a person, or in relation to our purposes, acquiring *ubuntu*. The first sense of morality revolves around the agent and the positive use of their agency. The first sense of morality is the same as what we referred to as the final good, or the "ought" part of the "ought implies can" principle. The first sense of morality involves the kind of moral value we acquire and one that we can also lose depending on our conduct. The second sense of morality focuses on certain capacities of the agent's metaphysical make-up. The capacity-based sense of morality involves the mere possession of certain significant ontological capacities. The kind of value associated with the second sense of morality is one that we have because of being the kinds of things that we are. We do not earn it, and we cannot lose; it is a function of our metaphysical make-up. The second sense of morality can be associated with an account of moral status.

The preceding quotation merely distinguishes the two senses of morality. In another place, Gyekye (1992: 111, emphasis mine) connects the two senses of morality; he does so by arguing that the agent-centred and the capacity-based connect or imply each other, which view (of African ethics) is consistent with our strategy of deriving moral status (capacity-based morality) from the final good (action- or agent-centred morality):

> The foregoing discussion of some morally significant expressions in the Akan language or judgements made about the conduct of persons suggests a conception of moral personhood; *a person is defined in terms of moral qualities or capacities*: a human person is a being who has a moral sense and is capable of making moral judgements.
> (Gyekye, 1992: 111, emphasis mine)

Keep in mind the distinction between the agent-centred and capacity-based senses of morality. Earlier, we quoted Gyekye distinguishing the two distinct senses of morality. In this quotation, Gyekye goes beyond merely distinguishing the agent from the capacity-based approach to morality; he posits a relationship between these two senses of morality. In his view, in keeping with our interpretation of the "ought implies can" principle, he argues that the agent-centred morality, the "ought" part, presupposes the capacity-based sense of morality, the "can" part. His line of reasoning is that the judgements we make about the agent's conduct (normative personhood) actually imply a capacity-based concept of morality, which he describes in terms of *moral personhood*. Notice that Gyekye defines moral personhood in terms of *certain qualities* or *capacities*. Moral personhood, defined in terms of moral qualities or capacities, has nothing to do with conduct; the mere possession of capacities is sufficient for it. Gyekye's point is straightforward – the pursuit of *ubuntu* or personhood as something that we ought to achieve has a metaphysical basis, which are certain qualities or capacities.

The distinction between the agent- and capacity-based approaches to morality, on the one hand, and the claim that the latter requires or presupposes the latter, on the other, lends support to the basic structure of our argument that we can reasonably presume or infer a conception of a capacity-based theory from the agent-centred theory. Commitment in Ubuntu thinkers that moral agents ought to pursue virtue or develop an empathetic disposition must have an ontological basis, and it is this presumption that we invoke to account for moral status in terms of the capacity for empathy. Hence, we conclude that an Ubuntu-based theory of moral status accounts for it in terms of the capacity for empathy.

Conclusion

The chapter articulated an Ubuntu-based account of moral status. It relied on the two components of Ubuntu ethics, the ontological and normative concepts of personhood. It associated the normative concept of personhood with the final good and the ontological concept with moral status. Using the "ought implies can" principle, it inferred a conception of moral status from the final good. The final good of *ubuntu*, which we interpreted in terms of developed empathy, represents the "ought" part of the "ought implies can" principle. An account of moral status that corresponds with the "can" part of the "ought implies can" principle is a function of the metaphysical capacity that undergirds our ability to fulfil the demands or prescriptions of morality. We account for moral status in terms of the capacity for *ubuntu* or, more accurately, in terms of the capacity for empathy. Hence, we conclude that human beings have moral status (or human dignity or are morally special) because they have the capacity for empathy. Moreover, the pursuit of *ubuntu* involves the development or cultivation of the capacity for empathy, which tends to express itself via altruism.

The next chapter defends the empathy-based interpretation of Ubuntu thinking.

Notes

1 Note that we do not focus on the last instance of the word *person*, or the phrase "through other persons", because it falls outside of the scope of our goal of inferring an account of moral status from the final good. The phrase "through other persons" draws our attention to the means through which ubuntu or one can become a person, social relationships.
2 Keep in mind also that the target of the agent's efforts is the development of the inner property/quality of her nature, which, when successful, will amount to her having *ubuntu*.
3 The suggestion we wish to make is that being humane is equivalent to altruism, which we believe has a place in Ubuntu thinking, but empathy is much more fundamental, and it is empathy that lies at the core of ubuntu, and empathy bolsters and triggers being humane (or altruism).
4 In a very powerful paper, Thaddeus Metz (2013) responds and criticizes Masolo's and Wiredu's interpretation of African ethics. Masolo and Wiredu define the final good in African ethics in terms of human well-being. Metz offers two compelling reasons that such an interpretation of African ethics is inadequate, particularly as the final good. For our purposes, we believe that one such argument will give the reader

a sense of why we reject well-being as the final. Imagine a case of an individual who stays in their own flat and they love watching other people when they bathe. They have all the sophisticated technology to do so. We stipulate that the victims of his invasive eye will never know about the onlooker. Our intuition seems to suggest that the onlooker is doing something wrong; he is violating a person in a very fundamental way, which we could explain in terms of the importance of privacy or even human dignity. Notice, however, that it seems we cannot say that the well-being, understood as a quality of life, of the "victim" has been undermined in any way. He will go on with his life as normal and his well-being intact. Well-being seems to fail to account for the wrong in such situation, which suggests its inadequacy as the final good.

References

Behrens, K. (2013). Two 'normative' conceptions of personhood. *Quest* 25: 103–119.
Biko, S. (2004). *I Write What I Like: a selection of his writings*. Johannesburg: Picador Africa.
Etieyibo, E. (2017). Ubuntu, Cosmopolitanism, and Distribution of Natural Resources. *Philosophical Papers* 46: 139–162.
Gyekye, K. (1997). *Tradition and Modernity*. New York: Oxford University Press.
Gyekye, K. (2010). African Ethics. In E. N. Zalta (Ed.), *The Stanford Encyclopedia of Philosophy*. http://plato.stanford.edu/archives/fall2011/entries/african-ethics (accessed 16 January 2013).
Horsthemke, K. (2015). *Animals and African Ethics*. New York, NY: Palgrave Macmillan.
Ikuenobe, P. (2017). The communal basis for moral dignity: an African perspective. *Philosophical Papers* 45: 437–469.
Kerr, B., Godfrey-Smith, P., Feldman, MW. (2004). What is altruism? *Trends Ecol Evol* 19: 135–40.
Korsgaard, C. (1983). Two Distinctions in Goodness. *Philosophical Review* 92: 169–195.
LenkaBula, P. (2008). Beyond anthropocentricity-Botho/Ubuntu and the quest for economic and ecological justice. Relig Theol 15:375–394.
Luthans, F., R. Van Wyk and F. O. Walumbwa. (2004). Recognition and Development of Hope for South African Organizational Leaders, The Leadership & Organization Development Journal 25: 512–527.
Lutz, D. (2009). African Ubuntu Philosophy and Global Management. *Journal of Business Ethics* 84: 13–328.
Masolo, D. (2004). Western and African Communitarianism: A Comparison. In K. Wiredu, (Eds.), *Companion to African Philosophy* 483–498 Oxford: Blackwell Publishing.
Masolo, D. (2010). *Self and Community in a Changing World*. Indianapolis: Indiana University Press.
Matolino, B., and W. Kwindingwi. (2013). The End of Ubuntu. *South African Journal of Philosophy* 32 (2): 197–205.
Menkiti, I. (1984). Person and community in African traditional thought. In: Wright, RA. (Ed.), *African philosophy: an introduction*. University Press of America, Lanham, pp 171–181.
Metz, T. (2007). Toward an African Moral Theory. *The Journal of Political Philosophy* 15: 321–341.

Metz, T. (2013). Two Conceptions of African Ethics in the Work of D. A. Masolo. *Quest* 25: 141–162.
Mokgoro, Y. (1998). Ubuntu and the Law in South Africa. *Potchefstroom Electronic Law Journal* 1: 1–11.
Molefe, M. (2017). A Critique of Thad Metz's African Theory of Moral Status. *South African Journal of Philosophy* 36 (2): 195–205.
Molefe, M. (2019). Ubuntu Ethics. *International Encyclopedia of Ethics*. DOI: 10.1002/9781444367072.wbiee936 (accessed 20 February 2021).
Molefe, M. (2021). *Partiality and Impartiality in African Philosophy*. New York: Lexington Books.
Molema, S. M. (1920). *The Bantu: Past and Present*, Edinburgh: W. Green and Son.
Munyaka, M., & Motlhabi, M. (2009). Ubuntu and Its Socio-Moral Significance. In F. Murove (Ed.), *African Ethics: An Anthology of Comparative and Applied Ethics*. Pietermaritzburg: University of KwaZulu Natal Press, 324–331.
Murove, F. (2014). Ubuntu. *Diogenes* 59: 36–47.
Ngcoya, M. (2015). 'Ubuntu: Toward an Emancipatory Cosmopolitanism?' *International Political Sociology* 9: 248–262.
Nyasani, J. (1989). The Ontological Significance of 'I' and 'We' in African Philosophy. In H. Kimmerle (Ed.), *I, We and Body: First Joint Symposium of Philosophers from Africa and from the Netherlands*. Amsterdam: B. R. Grüner, 9–16.
Okeja, U. (2013). *Normative Justification of a Global Ethic: A Perspective from African Philosophy*. New York: Lexington Books.
Oyowe, A. (2013). Strange bedfellows: Rethinking ubuntu and human rights in South Africa. *African Human Rights Law Journal* 13: 01–22.
Ramose, M. (1999). *African Philosophy Through Ubuntu*. Harare, Zimbabwe: Mond Books.
Ramose, M. (2003). The Ethics of Ubuntu. In P. Coetzee & A. Roux (Eds.), *The African Philosophy Reader*. New York: Routledge, 324–331.
Sherman, N. (1998). Empathy and Imagination. *Midwest Studies in Philosophy* 22: 82–118.
Shutte, A. (2001). *Ubuntu: An Ethic for the New South Africa*. Cape Town: Cluster Publications.
Shutte, A. (2009). Ubuntu as the African Ethical Vision. In Munyaradzi Felix Murove, (Ed.), *African Ethics: An Anthology for Comparative and Applied Ethics*, 85–99. University of KwaZulu-Natal Press.
Slote, M. (2007). *The Ethics of Care and Empathy*. New York: Routledge.
Slote, M. (2010). *Moral Sentimentalism*. New York: Oxford University Press.
Sober, E. (1991). What is Evolutionary Altruism? *Canadian Journal of philosophy* 18: 75–99.
Tutu, D. (1999). *No Future Without Forgiveness*. London: Rider.
Wall, S. (2012). Perfectionism in Moral and Political Philosophy. In *Stanford Encyclopaedia of Philosophy*. http://plato.stanford.edu/archives/win2012/entries/perfectionism-moral/ (accessed 10 March 2019).
Wiredu, K. (1992). Moral Foundations of an African Culture. In K. Wiredu & K. Gyekye (Eds.), *Person and Community: Ghanaian Philosophical Studies*, vol. 1. Washington, DC: The Council for Research in Values and Philosophy, 192–206.
Wiredu, K. (1996). *Cultural Universals and Particulars: An African Perspective*. Indianapolis: Indiana University Press.
Wiredu, K. (2009). An Oral Philosophy of Personhood: Comments on Philosophy and Orality. *Research in African Literatures* 40: 8–18.

4 Ubuntu, Empathy, and Moral Status

Introduction

This chapter proffers a preliminary defence of an empathy-based interpretation of Ubuntu ethics. The defence is twofold. First, we provide *prima facie* considerations that support the suitability of empathy to capture the essence of Ubuntu ethics. We will do so by demonstrating a fit between empathy and some characteristic ontological and axiological features of Ubuntu thinking. Second, we will provide prima facie consideration that supports the plausibility of an empathy-based account of moral status. To marshal a defence of an empathy-based interpretation of Ubuntu ethics, the chapter will comprise three sections. Each section will serve as a build-up towards a defence of an empathy-based interpretation of African ethics. The first section will give a definition of *empathy*. Here, we will clarify that we work with a definition of empathy, which, at its core, we understand to involve the fundamental ability to understand, to identify (or connect) with another, and to show concern towards them. The second section will motivate why we consider empathy a cornerstone of Ubuntu ethics. Here, we will demonstrate that there is a fit between empathy and what Ubuntu prescribes as an essential component of African ethical theory. Finally, we will further suggest the robustness of the empathy-based account of moral status by comparing it against Thaddeus Metz's friendliness account of moral status. We select Metz's friendliness theory because it is probably the most influential account of moral status in Ubuntu thinking.

We clarify and justify what we mean by a "preliminary defence" of an empathy-based account of African ethics. The defence that we will offer is preliminary in two senses in relation to both the literature on empathy and that on Ubuntu. First, the defence is preliminary in relation to the justification of an *empathy*-based interpretation of African ethics. There is vast literature with competing interpretations of the concept of empathy, spanning works in psychology, anthropology, philosophy, social work, and anthropology, among others. We are aware that even among philosophers, there is still much philosophical work that we still need to do to clarify and justify our own interpretation of empathy, given that it is both a popular and highly contested concept (Barnes, 2014). The defence of an empathy-based account is preliminary in this book in that we do not have space to develop a fully-fledged account of empathy against a thoroughgoing survey of competing conceptions of it and further justify why our own account is better. Rather, in proffering a preliminary defence, we are content to give the reader *a* picture of how empathy can inform a novel interpretation of an Ubuntu-inspired moral theory. We hope this picture will motivate others (and ourselves) to do extensive work on empathy in relation to African thought.[1]

Second, the defence is preliminary in relation to the literature on Ubuntu. There is an extensive body of literature that proposes competing interpretations of African ethics. Space will not permit us to explore all of them philosophically and to further justify the view that the empathy-based interpretation is the most plausible. To give the reader *prima facie* consideration of why they ought to take the empathy interpretation of Ubuntu seriously, we will contrast our view against one influential interpretation of it in the literature, Metz's friendliness interpretation of African ethics. We will point out that empathy view does better than friendliness in securing the intuition that severely mentally incapacitated individuals have greater moral status than (all) animals. This comparison will surely not be sufficient to demonstrate the plausibility of an empathy-based account; however, it goes somewhere in suggesting that it is an underexplored theoretical option that has been overlooked and ignored in the literature and warrants serious consideration.[2]

In what follows we define *empathy*.

What Is Empathy?

We note that empathy is a contested concept. Note the comment about its contested status:

> There are different meanings [of empathy] within each particular context of its use. . . . Thus, despite the confusion that emerges in relation to "what it is," many have embraced empathy's multiplicity. Indeed, there are almost as many definitions of empathy as people studying it.
> (Barnes, 2014: 561–562)

We stipulate an understanding of empathy that we consider suitable for purposes of contributing towards an African ethical theory, or Ubuntu thinking. Before we stipulate our definition of empathy, analyse its elements, and consider its implications for morality, the reader should note the following two considerations. First, we draw and associate our definition of empathy within the literature from eighteenth-century sentimentalists, modern psychology studies (such as Batson, 2012), and contemporary (sentimentalist) moral theories (such as Slote, 2007) that associate it with certain altruistic (or caring) or pro-social behaviours. The point of departure is that on our view, empathy essentially involves a motivation and disposition to help another person (which we describe in terms of altruism, or care), which view is described in the literature as the empathy–altruism hypothesis. Second, we draw from and associate our definition of empathy with literature that tends to defend the view that there is a necessary relationship between empathy and morality. Specifically, we consider literature that defends "proper empathy" or "fully developed empathy" or any such related phrases, which propose a concept of empathy, as a virtue, which is relevant in a moral theory (Carse, 2005: 169; Simmons, 2014; Song, 2015: 437). We understand proper empathy or developed to involve three components, the epistemic, relational, and a caring disposition.

At its core, empathy involves having a "matching" or "similar" emotion or feeling with another person because s/he has the same feeling (Snow, 2000: 69). If a person feels sad because they have lost their loved one, one empathizes with her in as far as they also feel sad because she feels sad for having lost her loved one. Empathy, in this sense, involves emotional sharing or having (more or less) a similar inner experience that is essential to what is involved in empathizing with another (Song, 2015). We understand empathy to have both cognitive and affective (emotional sharing) aspects, that is, empathy involves the "mentalizing" and "affect sharing" components (Barnes, 2014: 561). The cognitive component involves the analysis and evaluation of another person and her situation, which leads to the recognition, belief, or awareness that s/he is experiencing a particular emotion (Barnes, 2014). Snow (2000: 71) notes that "[i]f we do not believe that the other experiences (an) emotion, then, by definition, we cannot empathize" with her. The affective experience involves the agent experiencing a matching feeling or emotion of the object of empathy from the awareness that she is experiencing it (Simmons, 2014).

First, we note that empathy involves recognizing the distinction between the self and other. The self feels a matching emotion, which is caused by the other, who is experiencing the emotion. The self's internal experience tracks and reflects the internal experience of another (Decety & Jackson, 2004).[3] Second, we note developed or proper empathy, which captures it as a virtue suitable to respond to the human condition of need and involves three elements, namely, the epistemic component, the relational component, and the empathy–altruism hypothesis (Simmons, 2014). The epistemic component is crucial in helping moral agents be able to make correct or "wise moral decisions in particular contexts" (2005: 171). Empathy is the mode of knowing other minds; specifically, it facilitates a deep and first-person understanding of the inner experience of another person. Sherman (1998: 89), drawing from Adam Smith's account of empathy, sheds light on the kind of understanding associated with empathy:

> Smith suggests the task is even more robust – to become the other person – to "enter, as it were, into his body and become in some measure the same

person with him". . . . . It is as if I not only change circumstances with you, but I change persons and character. Here, it is not simply the external perspective or situation that is key to imaginative transport but the taking on of another's internal dispositions and attitudes.

Empathy-based understanding at least has two features. On the one hand, the subject of empathy brackets herself, her experiences, and her standpoint to give centre stage to the object of empathy (Snow, 2000). On the other hand, empathy-based understanding involves sharing in another's emotional experience from her own internal perspective grounded on her disposition, motivation, and attitudes. Simmons (2014: 104) remarks that empathy-based understanding also includes "experience(ing) the others' purposes from her perspective, seeing and feeling the other's purposes as she sees and feels them. The other experiences her purposes as worthwhile important, meaningful, and mattering, as worthy of being fulfilled". Morality requires that we have correct knowledge of the moral object if we are to respond correctly to the human condition.

The relational component, according to Song (2015), has three elements that characterize it, namely, *company*, *acknowledgement*, and *responsiveness*. Company involves a special kind of being with another characterized by sharing something that is "meaningful" – the object of empathy's internal experience, that is, viewing and experiencing the world from their emotional standpoint and perspective (447). Song correctly observes that "what matters most to us is what we think, feel, care about and aspire to, we feel deeper company when our internal life, more than anything else, is shared by another person" (447). Acknowledgement involves recognizing and affirming the subjectivity of the object of empathy without necessarily endorsing how she feels. It is acknowledging another, rather than ignoring her, which is another connecting element of empathy, where the subject of empathy affirms the other's inner experience rather than merely dismissing it. One might be unjustified in being disappointed for not getting the job while there are good reasons why she did not get it. One could hold the view that it is fair that she did not get the job while still acknowledging her feelings of disappointment. Responsiveness involves responding correctly to another, sensitive to how they may receive the response or reactions, to facilitate connection between the subject and object of empathy. Empathy involves "fine-tuning her response so that it 'speaks to' the other, in addition to addressing her situation" (2015: 448). Therefore, one of the ways to connect to another is by responding to her in ways that are consistent with her internal experience, her purposes, and what matters to her.

The final aspect of proper empathy or developed empathy involves the empathy–altruism hypothesis. The empathy–altruism hypothesis posits a correlation between empathy and altruism (and care). We consider altruism (or care) to involve "*concerned support, intervention, nurturance, or guidance*" (Carse, 2005: 170). It is the element of altruism that explains the truckload of pro-social attitudes and behaviours associated with empathy. In our view, proper empathy or full empathy involves understanding another's internal experience, point of view, and what matters to her (epistemic dimension); the rich relationships we could have with others (characterized by the connecting elements of company, acknowledgement, and responsiveness) and the element care (or altruism) that involves nurturing, support, or intervention to the human condition of need. Hence, we note that the epistemic and relational components of empathy teach us something about being human-with-another; moreover, it has the potential to enrich our human lives as individuals and our relationships by helping us escape the ego-centric perspective and to put us in a position to relate, interpret, and support another from her own emotional standpoint (Sherman, 1998). When I feel what you are feeling, and I also consider your feelings and purpose as mattering for their own sake and important to you, I should be disposed and motivated to help you, at least to some extent, particularly if it is possible and it does not require me to make extraordinary sacrifices. On our view, proper empathy or developed empathy involves understanding, relationality, and care.[4]

We turn next to motivating for the suitability of empathy.

Motivation for the Suitability of Empathy

This section justifies empathy as the defining essence of Ubuntu ethics. In this view, having *ubuntu* is the same as having developed empathy. We understand developed empathy to have three central components, the epistemic aspect (which involves understanding another), the relational component (which involves connecting with another), and the caring aspect (which involves intervening to support, nurture, or guide another). Empathy involves engaging with another in a way that recognizes, affirms, and empowers them. We will justify the suitability of empathy by demonstrating that it is consistent with the ontological and axiomatic assumptions characteristic of African thought. First, we will note that empathy is consistent with the ontological conception of what it means to be human, and it plays a crucial role in accounting for the socialization of human beings as social beings. Second, we note that the essence of African ontology and ethics resides in the view that human beings are essentially inadequate, vulnerable, and will always need the help of fellow human beings. In this regard, we will show how empathy best helps us relate (identify) and respond to the human condition of need. Finally, we will also show how empathy can account for the moral-political axiom associated with the common good, or the idea of consensus. We argue that the fit between empathy and these three conditions, or considerations, justify its suitability in accounting for African ethics or Ubuntu thinking.

Human Relationality and Empathy

We invoke empathy because it can explain the relational or social conception of human nature. In this sense, we argue that empathy provides the onto-psychological content to the ontological view that human nature is relational by nature, that is, it explains how we are relational, as suggested by African thought. The idea of relationality, construed ontologically, amounts to the view that being human involves being in relationships with others. The aphorisms characteristic of African moral thought and/or Ubuntu thinking lend support to the relational conception of human nature: "I am because we are" and "a person is a person through other persons".

The "I am" part refers to the individual component, and the "we are" part refers to the relational component of what it means to be human. The relational component, the "we are" part, indicates that in the absence of social relationships with others, there is no possibility for the emergence of the human subject. Hence, on this view, to be human, biologically, psychologically, culturally, and morally, cannot emerge outside of the "because we are" or without "other persons". Menkiti (2004: 324) rightly interprets the aphorism "I am because we are" to refer to an individual

> who recognizes the sources of his or her own humanity, and so realizes, within internal assurance, that in the absence of others, no grounds exist for a claim regarding the individual's own standing as a person. The notion at work here is the notion of an extended self.

Menkiti's thought, put positively, amounts to the view that the source and continuance for the emergence and function of the human subject is possible only in the context of social relationships with others. Dzobo (1992: 132) affirms the relationality of being human by use of the analogy of a coal when he avers that "[a]s the glow of a coal depends upon its remaining in the fire, so the vitality, the psychic security, the very humanity of man, depends on his integration" on social relationships with other human beings.

We posit that empathy is the psycho-relational mechanism that facilitates human interaction and connection, which plays a crucial role in the socialization, humanization, and well-functioning of human beings. Hence, Menkiti talks of an "extended self," where the human subject/agent empathetically perceives herself through, in, and with others (ibid.). At the very root of what it means to be human is the ability to identify and connect with others. This ability, empathy, is responsible for the emergence and normal development of the human subject. That is, empathy could be considered to be the very psychological mechanism, or glue, that facilitates human connection in its various manifestations in human functioning. Decety and Cowell (2014: 526) argue that "empathy plays an essential role in interpersonal relations, including early attachment between primary caregiver and child, caring for the well-being of others, and facilitating cooperation". Stueber (2019: n.p., emphasis mine) also avers that empathy "is used to refer to a wide range of psychological capacities that are thought of as being central for constituting humans as *social creatures* allowing us to know what other people are thinking and feeling".

It is in this sense that we believe that empathy can enrich discourses on African ontological and normative thought in relation to the tendency to place a prime on social relationships and the community. Empathy, as a psycho-social mechanism, and the capacities associated with it, could play a crucial role in explaining human relationality, interpersonal relationships, relational autonomy, intersubjectivity, and the idea of community, which scholars of Africa have merely taken for granted, but have not considered psycho-social resources to account for this important element of human sociality. If Wiredu (1996) is correct to argue that there is a biological basis for the emergence of the brain, communication, and our sociality, it seems empathy could be the resource that plays a crucial role in serving as the basis of a crucial aspect of African ontological thought, which we believe justifies its suitability in African thought.

Human Need and Empathy

The second ontological basis, which connects with the first axiomatic assumption of African axiological thought that we believe justifies the suitability of empathy, is the human condition of need, dependence, and vulnerability. African moral thought operates on the assumption that certain ontological facts connected with the human condition ground and justify morality. For example, Gyekye (1992) argues that certain conceptions of human nature inform ethics and politics. Moreover, the tendency by scholars of African ethics to insist on ethical humanism proceeds from the assumption that certain ontological features of human nature ground morality (see Molefe, 2015). One such human condition is the view that human beings are perpetually in a state of vulnerability, inadequacy, and need, in one way or another.[5] In the context of explaining the ontological inadequacy of human beings, Wiredu (1992: 201) notes, "This imperative (to help others) is born of an acute sense of the essential dependency of the human condition. The idea of dependency may even be taken as a component of the Akan conception of a person". The idea of dependency is the ontological condition of what it means to be human. Like feminist or care ethics, African moral thought is grounded in the ontological view that human nature is perpetually insufficient and vulnerable (see Miller, 2014; Molefe & Allsobrook, 2021).

We can distinguish at least two kinds of needs associated with human nature, namely, well-being and moral needs. Well-being needs are those connected to biological sustenance, and moral needs are those associated with the sociomoral-political resources the agent requires to be able to meaningfully participate in morality (Hamilton, 2003). Living in a condition of perpetual poverty signifies the lack of access to well-being needs. Lack of access to freedom to act out one's will reflects a lack of sociomoral-political needs. Odera Oruka's (1997) talk of the *human minimum* emerges precisely to capture and respond to the human condition of need. "Human minimum" refers to a package of basic goods and resources, basic needs, which every human being must have access to for them to lead a satisfactory human life, which for Oruka (the human minimum) consists of *subsistence, health,* and *security* (ibid.). Without the provision of basic human needs (whatever they may be), the possibility for the emergence of a robust human agent is in jeopardy.

We propose empathy as a suitable candidate to account for Ubuntu thinking precisely because it has resources that fit in directly with the ontological condition of need and the requirement to show concern or sensitivity to the human condition of need. We noted that empathy has the epistemic and relational components. These two dimensions are crucial in that they facilitate understanding of another's condition of need (from their internal point of view) and a meaningful connection with another (where the empathizer shares in her emotions, acknowledges her emotions, and responds to them from her standpoint). This approach is better than Wiredu's (1996) golden rule approach to respond to the human condition of need. Whereas the golden rule requires that we should do onto others as we would that they do to us, where what the agent thinks and feels is good takes centre stage in determining her response to the object of moral concern. Empathy, on the other hand, requires us to temporarily suspend ourselves (our ideas, feelings, desires, and so on) as the centre of attention, and it demands of us to understand the world, internally (emotional experience of another, their feelings, desires, ideas, and so on) and externally (situations in the world). It is the experience and perspective of the one in need that becomes the point of reference and focus. That is, I do not relate with you on the basis of what I think is best for you; rather, I relate with you mindful of what you think and believe is best for you.

Moreover, the relevance of empathy is further justified by its capacity to respond to the human condition of need. Empathy is apt to respond to human condition, at least in our interpretation of it, since we consider it to be tethered to altruism (or care), that is, we construe empathy to trigger altruism. Like Sherman (1998: 82), in a different context, we posit that "at a minimum, I shall argue that a viable conception of altruistic virtue presupposes the capacity for empathetic" concern, imagination, and sharing. The function of empathy in triggering altruism (or care) is crucial in that it expresses itself via other-regarding attitudes and conduct aimed to nurture, support, and empower another person. The empathy-triggered altruism further fits with one of the ethical axioms of African thought. The ethical axiom (that is prompted by the perpetual state of inadequacy and vulnerability associated with human nature) states that "showing sensitivity to the needs of others is an *important plank* in the ethical platform of communitarianism" (Gyekye, 1992: 172, emphasis mine). Metz (2007: 326, emphasis mine), in his analysis of some of the fundamental moral intuitions of African thought, remarks:

> A greater percentage of Africans think that one is morally obligated to help others, roughly to the extent that one can and *that others need*, with rights not figuring into the analysis of how much one ought to transfer wealth, time or labour.

Consistently, the literature in African ethics insists on the view that to have *ubuntu*, or to be a person, revolves around a character disposition that is sensitive and responsive to the needs of others (see Wiredu, 1992; Gyekye, 1997; Masolo, 2004; Metz, 2007; Munyaka & Motlhabi, 2009; Etieyibo, 2017).

The plausibility of empathy-triggered altruism is recommended by its fit with this axiom that requires agents to recognize another's humanity and needs that essentially characterize it. Empathy is justified because it is able to theoretically explain and justify why we should take this ethical axiom in African thought seriously. The natural and persistent state of insufficiency, vulnerability, and dependence justifies the ethical imperative that "[h]uman beings, therefore, at all times, in one way or another, directly or indirectly, need the help of their kind" (1992: 202). We argue that empathy-triggered altruism gives us a theoretically underexplored way to account for morality as geared towards responding to the condition of human need through empathy, and it theoretically explains the idea of helping fellow human beings through empathy that triggers altruism. If morality is about the human condition of need and African ethics requires us to show sensitivity and be responsive to need, then empathy and its correlation to altruism is consistent with this requirement, which justifies its suitability.

The Common Good, Consensus, and Empathy

We have already connected empathy with human relationality and the human condition of vulnerability (or need). We now proceed to justify the suitability of empathy to account for Ubuntu thinking by considering its fit with another crucial axiom of African moral and political thought. The maxim finds expression in two common ways. On the one hand, scholars talk of the *common good* as a central plank of African moral-political thought. On the other hand, scholars of African thought recommend the value and practice of consensus as the essence or even the means to secure the common good. The "common good" refers to a basket of goods and basic needs that human beings require to lead a satisfactory life (Gyekye, 1997). Wiredu explains the idea of the common good in African thought by appealing to the art form of the crocodile with two heads and one stomach. He comments as follows regarding this art form:

> Among the Akans, some of the most profound philosophic conceptions are expressed by art motifs, and a celebrated answer to this question is offered in one such construct of fine art: a crocodile with one stomach and two heads locked in combat. Lessons: (1) Although human beings have a core of common interests, they also have conflicting interests that precipitate real struggles. (2) The aim of morality, as also derivatively of statesmanship, is to harmonize those warring interests through systematic adjustment and adaptation. The one stomach symbolizes not only the commonality of interests but also a natural basis for the possibility of a solution to the existential antinomy.
>
> (1992: 186)

The question that Wiredu is attempting to answer by appealing to the art form concerns the justification of moral rules in our social existence. He believes that the art form has profound philosophical conceptions in relation to the justification of moral rules. For him, the art form captures three crucial considerations. The first is, as represented by the single stomach, the common good. The second, as represented by the two heads, is the real struggle or conflict among moral agents in trying to satisfy their interests. The final aspect, which is related to the preceding aspects, is that the essence of morality revolves around systematically harmonizing warring interests, which threaten the common good. At this point, Wiredu captures the axiom associated with ethics and politics, the belief that *there is a natural basis for the possibility of a solution to the existential antinomy*. This natural basis for securing the common good is conceptualized and operationalized in the literature on African philosophy in terms of the concept of *consensus*. There is an agreement in the literature that consensus is an axiomatic assumption of African ethical thought (Gyekye, 1992; Wamala, 2004; Teffo, 2004; Ramose, 2009). Wiredu (1995: 53, emphasis mine) makes the following remark in relation to consensus:

> Let us note an important fact about the role of consensus in African life. The reliance on consensus is not a peculiarly political phenomenon. Where consensus characterizes political decision-making in Africa, it is a manifestation of an *immanent approach to social interaction*. Generally, *in interpersonal relations among adults, consensus as a basis of joint action was taken as axiomatic*. This is not to say that it was always attained.

The point that we are making is that African moral thought is characterized by certain fundamental moral assumptions or beliefs, which we may even describe as axiomatic. In this instance, we have two such related axiomatic assumptions, the belief that we have at core common interests (the common good) and the belief that consensus is or ought to be a defining feature of interpersonal relations of all kinds from friends and family to the various subsidiaries of the state.

In relation to consensus, we believe empathy, as the ability to identify and connect with others, is consistent with this goal and will be very useful in a cultural and axiological context that operates based on consensus. Empathy, the willingness to put oneself in another person's shoes, promises – note, we did not say it guarantees – to effectively contribute towards the attainment of reconciliation and to foster solidarity in decision-making. In attempting to reconcile warring interests/views and bridging the gap between diverging perspectives, empathy could be a useful psycho-social mechanism to facilitate the appreciation of each other's differing viewpoints *en route* to a compromise or reconciled view. We believe that empathy is compatible with African ethics, or Ubuntu thinking's emphasis on harmony, solidarity, and consensus. It can serve as a useful psycho-moral tool to facilitate the achievement of harmony or consensus.

It is our view that Ubuntu ethics is characterized by the ontological assumption (human nature as relational and perpetually vulnerable) and the axiological axiomatic assumptions (showing sensitivity to the human condition of need and the commitment to securing the common good via the attitude and practice of consensus). It is in this light that we propose or argue that empathy is an underexplored, promising, and plausible interpretation of African ethics, or Ubuntu thinking, since it is consistent, or has a fit, with the ontological and axiomatic characteristics of it (African thought). We suggest that if our humanity is something that we acquire and share with others in social relationships, then empathy plays a crucial role in the emergence and functioning of the subject as a biological, cultural, and social being. We also suggested that empathy is crucial in that it is consistent with the two axioms of African moral thought, sensitivity to the human condition of need and the requirement of consensus for securing harmony among warring interests (as represented by the two heads in the moral contexts), in interpersonal relationships and in political and policy decision-making contexts. It is the potential resourcefulness of empathy that justifies it, at least at the prima facie level, as a promising psycho-moral concept, or even a virtue, to the interpretation of Ubuntu thinking.

Next, we proceed to contrast an empathy-based account of moral status against the friendliness account of moral status.

Empathy versus Friendliness as Accounts of Moral Status

To further motivate an empathy-based theory of moral status of Ubuntu ethics, I contrast it against the friendliness view of it. Thaddeus Metz defends what he considers a plausible Afro-communitarian moral theory based on Ubuntu thinking. He identifies at least six possible moral theories of African ethics, or Ubuntu ethics, and he ultimately defends the harmony-based account, which he also describes in terms of community, as the most plausible against other contenders, such as life, well-being, rights, personhood, and survival (Metz, 2007). In his initial statement of Ubuntu ethics, he considered harmonious relationships to be intrinsically good. In his revision of the theory, he considers not the communal or social relationships of harmony (or friendliness) to be intrinsically good; rather, he locates intrinsic goodness in the *capacity* for harmonious relationships (Metz, 2010, 2011). He argues that the most plausible way to interpret the characteristic feature of Ubuntu thinking, harmony or community, is to comprise two distinct relationships, the relationships of identity and solidarity (Metz, 2011, 2022). "Identity", roughly refers to sharing a way of life, where one thinks of personal identity in terms of we, where one shares common goals and collaborates with others to pursue the shared goals (Metz, 2022). "Solidarity" refers to empowering or benefitting another for their own sake (Metz, 2022). He argues that the combination of identity and solidarity amounts to "love" or, more accurately, "friendliness" (ibid., 67).

In this view, moral status is a function of the capacity for identity and solidarity, or simply, the capacity for friendliness. Metz describes his account of moral status as a "modal-relational" approach (Metz, 2022: 96). It is *modal-relational* in that it accounts for moral status in terms of the capacity to enter into relationships and not actually participating in them (Metz, 2012). Anything that has the capacity, all things being equal, to participate in friendly relations does have moral status, without regard to contingent obstacles that may, at that time, such as being drunk or temporarily comatose, obstruct its ability to do so (Metz, 2012). It is the mere possession of the relevant relational capacity that secures moral status. Metz further distinguishes between those entities that can both be subjects and objects of friendliness and those that can only be objects of such relationships. Those entities that can both be subjects and objects of friendliness have full moral status or human dignity. Those that can only be objects of friendly relations have partial moral status. In this view, normal adult human beings are paradigm cases of full moral status because they can initiate friendly relations, and they can also benefit, as objects, from friendly relations. Animals, on the other hand, have partial moral status because they can only be objects of friendly relations, at least according to Metz's view.

Contrary to the account of moral status that captures it in terms of the capacity for friendliness, we propose an empathy-based account of moral status. Like Metz's account of moral status, the empathy-based account of moral status is relational, that is, both of these accounts base moral status on the capacity to relate with others in a particular way. They differ, however, in two related ways. First, they differ in terms of the specification of the normatively relevant relationship. Metz proposes friendliness, and we propose empathy. Second, on Metz's account, it is either the possession of the relevant capacity (subject of friendliness) or the ability to be affected by the relationship that confers moral status (object of friendliness). On our part, we draw the distinction between full moral status and partial moral status differently. Any being that has the capacity for empathy has full moral status; any being that belongs to the community of beings that, by nature, have the capacity for moral status has partial moral status, which, however, is higher than that of any other being that can be an object of relations of empathy (but is not part of the human community). Although some human beings may lack empathy, they do have moral status, which is greater than that of animals, for example, that may only be objects of such relations.

We justify the higher moral status of entities that lack empathy but belong to the community of things that have such a nature by appealing to the idea of moral holism, which might be an instance of moral relationalism. Another manifestation of relationalism in African ontological and axiological thought is via a commitment to moral holism (Michel & Verhoef, 1997; Bujo, 2005; Behrens, 2011). Based on moral holism, an entity has moral status merely because it belongs to the relevant community of things with moral status (Dion, 1987). Belonging to such a natural community gives some moral status, without regard to it lacking capacities associated with that community, but not full moral status. Full moral status belongs only to those entities that actually possess the capacity for empathy. Put simply, those who can actually cultivate empathy or who possess the capacity for it have full moral status. Those that belong to the community of beings that can pursue *ubuntu*, that is, develop or cultivate empathy, but lack the metaphysical capacities to do so themselves have partial moral status for merely belonging to this community. We will justify this view on the basis of the logic of moral holism. Finally, those things that lack the capacity for empathy, to the threshold manifested in relation to the kind of epistemic and relational functions associated with it, but can be objects of it, such as animals, among others, have partial moral status.

The standard for considering whether an entity can be an object of empathy is just the fact that its well-being can be affected by withdrawing empathy-induced altruism or friendliness. Things that can be objects of empathy or even friendliness tend to be characterized by the property of sentience in as far as their lives can be better or worse off (see Metz, 2012). It is this minimum standard of well-being that we use to consider whether an entity can be an object of empathy or friendliness.

With this rough sketch of both the friendliness and empathy accounts of moral status, we can proceed to evaluate both theories. Space will not allow us to perform an extensive comparison of both theories of moral status. To demonstrate the ground of why we are suggesting that the empathy-based account of moral status warrants serious consideration, we will compare both accounts in relation to the problem associated with the argument from marginal cases, hence AMC (Singer, 2009). We believe that AMC will serve as a suitable test case to demonstrate the promise of the empathy-based account of moral status.

The Moral Status of Marginal Cases

The common assumption in moral philosophy is that all human beings have equal moral status and that moral status is greater than that of animals. It is these assumptions that animate scholars to object to these assumptions by appeal to cases of people in the margins, that is, at least in this instance, those that are severely mentally incapacitated (henceforth, SMI). The essence of AMC is expressed as follows:

> If one truly believes that so-called "marginal" humans, such as the retarded or the senile, have basic moral rights, it was urged, then one must grant that nonhumans at the same level of mental development as these humans possess basic moral rights too. To accept moral status for the first group while denying it to the second is to be guilty of outright moral inconsistency.
> (Pluhar, 1987: 23)

On AMC, some animals appear to have at least equal, if not greater, moral status than most marginal cases because they have equal or greater cognitive abilities than most marginal cases, supposing we stipulate rationality as the standard for moral status. A normal adult gorilla has superior cognitive abilities compared to SMI. Metz (2022: 157) argues that his theory is able to successfully respond to AMC. He promises to explain "why a severely mentally incapacitated human being might have a greater moral status than an animal with identical internal feature". (He wants to defend (some version of) the common intuition in moral philosophy, which intuition we also share and is prevalent in African moral thought that human beings have greater moral status, including SMI, than animals.) He justifies this view by arguing that "the capacity (on the part of SMI) for being an object of a friendly relationship with us to a much greater degree than that had by other beings such as mice and elephants" (2022: 158). Why must we believe that SMI individuals have a higher degree of being objects of friendly relations, hence greater moral status, than animals with identical internal features? Metz provides the following as evidence:

> We do much more for the . . . (mentally) incapacitated than we do (for) animals, which is evidence of a greater ability to make them an object of a friendly relationship and hence a higher moral status than what animals have.
> (ibid.)

This argument is less than convincing for two reasons. First, it begs the question, Why should we believe that SMI persons have greater moral status than animals? To have greater moral status means exactly that we ought to do more for SCI than animals. To answer the question by appealing to the fact that we tend to do more for them as evidence that they have greater capacity to be objects of friendly relations strikes us as begging the question. We are asking the question precisely because we are questioning (given the concerns raised by AMC); we are justified to treat them as if they have the greater capacity to be objects of friendly relations. Put differently, we can pose the question in this fashion: Why must we do more for SCI than animals? The answer cannot be that because they have greater moral status. The answer must provide an explanation that goes beyond the question to give us an independent reason that we must hold that belief in the first place. Moreover, even if we accept as evidence (our doing more for the mentally incapacitated) of greater capacity to be objects of greater moral status than animals, this kind of evidence is less than convincing, at least as it stands.

Consider two cases. First, how do we convince people who tend to do more for animals than human beings that they are wrong? They might actually believe that it is easier for us to relate with animals than human beings. The second case involves the consideration that we tend for people with whom we share a special relationship, be it a friendship or romance – a case of moral partialism. Or consider a questionable case: racists tend to do more for their racial kind than they would for people from other races – a case of racism. We will agree that in all these cases, it does not follow that doing more for others is evidence of the moral patient's greater capacity to be an object of friendliness. Once again, a more convincing reason must appeal to some other, independent reason, from our actual treatment of severely mentally incapacitated, to justify why we must believe they have greater moral status than animals. As the theory stands, it does not give us a satisfactory response to the AMC.

On the empathy-based account of moral status, SCI persons have greater moral status than all nonhuman animals. Metz's view assigns greater moral status to severely mentally incapacitated persons against a subset of animals, which he defines in terms of having *identical internal features* with incapacitated persons. As far as I am aware, he does not specify these identical internal features or give us examples of animals that share such features with SMI. The implication of his view is that animals that may not have identical internal features may have greater moral status than severely mentally incapacitated persons, which indicates that Metz has ultimately not addressed the problem of marginal cases or the intuition that all human beings have greater moral status than animals.

The empathy-based account assigns greater moral status to all human beings compared to animals on two bases. On the one hand, normal adult human beings have dignity or full moral status because they have the capacity for empathy. On the other hand, severely mentally incapacitated individuals have greater moral status on the logic of moral holism. Moral holism assigns moral status not because of its internal capacity but in terms of its membership to a group with moral status (Metz, 2007: 333). That is, by merely belonging to the community of beings that have empathy, they enjoy a greater moral status than beings that do not belong to this community. We invoke holistic logic because it is a characteristic feature of African metaphysical and axiological thought. The hierarchy usually invoked to depict an African conception of reality and morality places all human beings above all animals and other existing things (Magesa, 1997; Metz, 2012). Human beings, by merely belonging in the human stratum in the hierarchy that is above the one occupied by animals, have greater moral status. The hierarchy operates on the logic of moral holism.

To secure the claim that SMI has greater moral status than all animals may be resisted by some because it hangs on a controversial metaphysical system to account for moral holism, which may not have a strong appeal to secular and modern societies when developing bioethical policies. We insist that the basic insight behind moral holism that species have moral status comparative or proportional to their group can be defended by appealing to metaphysical approaches by comparable secular accounts. We will invoke one such metaphysical approach to bolster and illuminate the empathy-based account of moral status. Consider Daniel Sulmasy (2009) in the bioethical context of discussing the importance of moral status and/or intrinsic dignity. *Intrinsic dignity* refers to a value that is inherent in a particular entity because it is the kind of thing it is. The idea of "the kind of thing it is" signals the metaphysical idea of a natural kind. Instead of explaining the reality in the world in terms of a quasireligious metaphysical hierarchy, we can appeal to the idea of natural kinds to justify why SCIs have greater moral status than animals. Sulmasy's (2009: 477, emphasis mine) comment on natural kinds and dignity is illuminating:

> Intrinsic value, to repeat, is the value something has by virtue of being the kind of thing that it is. Thus, the intrinsic value of a natural entity – the value it has by virtue of being the kind of thing that it is – *depends upon one's ability to pick that entity out as a member of a natural kind*. Intrinsic dignity, then, is the intrinsic value of entities that are members of a natural kind that is, as a kind, capable of language, rationality, love, free will, moral agency, creativity, aesthetic sensibility, and an ability to grasp the finite and infinite.

In this metaphysical and axiological scheme, natural kinds are characterized by certain features characteristic of their kind as a specific group distinct from other kinds that also have their own specific characteristic features. In this metaphysical view, the world is composed of natural kinds with their individual characteristic features. The intrinsic value, or moral status, of an individual entity is a function of it being a member of that natural kind. Sulmasy (2009: 477) proceeds to make the following comment that captures insight similar to what we call holistic logic in the natural kinds of metaphysical and ethical scheme:

> Importantly, the logic of natural kinds suggests that one picks individuals out as members of the kind not because they express all the necessary and sufficient predicates to be classified as a member of a species but, rather, by virtue of their inclusion under the extension of a natural kind that, as a kind, has those capacities.

On this view, by merely being a member of the natural kind, even though the individual does not possess all the necessary and sufficient properties typical of that kind, we should extend intrinsic value to her on the extensional logic. In this view, all entities belonging to a natural kind have moral status without regard to whether they possess all features typical of that species. The extensional inclusion grants SCI intrinsic value, or moral status. We can justify that SCI individuals have greater moral status than all animals on the basis of the secular and plausible metaphysical view of natural kinds as an account of things (species) in the world. Hence, we accept the insight of moral holism as represented in the African metaphysical hierarchy of reality, which assigns greater moral status on the basis of merely belonging to the human stratum. We suggest that the metaphysical view of natural kinds secures the intuition that all human beings, including SCI, have greater moral status than all animals without the baggage of a quasireligious metaphysical system.

If a plausible theory of moral status must be able to account for the persistent intuition that human beings have greater moral status than animals or solve the challenge raised in relation to the marginal cases, it follows that an empathy-based account appears to do better than the friendliness account. This comparison is not meant to suggest that the friendliness view is altogether implausible or that the empathy-based account is all-around plausible compared to the friendliness view. The point of this comparison was merely to indicate that it does have resources that warrant it being taken seriously as an interpretation of Ubuntu ethics. Hence, we only promised preliminary defence.

Conclusion

This chapter proffered a preliminary defence of an empathy-based interpretation of African ethics. It defended the promise of the empathy-based interpretation of Ubuntu ethics in two ways. First, we argued that empathy has resources that are consistent with some of the fundamental ontological and axiological assumptions characteristic of African ethics, or Ubuntu thinking, namely, the ontological condition of need, the axiological assumption of showing sensitivity and responsiveness to the human condition of need,

76 African Moral Philosophy

and the axiological assumption of consensus as the basis for managing interpersonal and political issues. Second, we compared the empathy-based and friendliness-based theories of moral status. We compared them in relation to the AMC, specifically, whether they can plausibly explain the moral intuition that human beings, specifically SCI, have greater moral status than animals. We argued that an empathy-based theory of moral status, on the face of it, does a better job than the friendliness account of it.

Next, we apply empathy-based theory to the bioethical question of euthanasia.

Notes

1 Molefe (2020) has begun suggesting that sympathy/empathy might be the way to go. In this book, however, we go a step further in connecting with a broader community of literature on empathy to consider how it might have a bearing on reimagining African ethics, or Ubuntu.
2 We motivate empathy as the basis to understand or construe Ubuntu thinking because it will force us to go beyond mere philosophical speculation to also consider empirical evidence concerning our biology, how it works, so that as much as we develop moral theories, to some extent, these moral theories will find some support in the science of morality.
3 The distinction between the self and other is important for several reasons. First, it clarifies that it is the internal worldview, inner experience, and her perception of it, and possibly her view of the external factors, which ought to be the point of focus when empathizing. Second, keeping the distinction clear is important also because it forestalls the dangers associated with empathy when it goes like self-effacement in the instance where one overidentifies to a point where they lose their own sense of self because they are engrossed with the other. Hence, empathy should be understood as a temporary bracketing of one's own desires, beliefs, and perspectives to identify with the other – the bracketing must be temporary so as not to lose a sense of self and integrity (Snow, 2000).
4 Several objections have been raised against empathy as the ground for morality in the literature in philosophy. The objections against the close connection between empathy and morality note "serious problems in our exercise of empathy – we are naturally biased, empathize too much or too little, and prone to making all sorts of mistakes in empathizing" (Song, 2014: 437). The literature also objects on empathy's status as virtue on the grounds "(1) that empathy is unnecessary for being ethical, (2) that it is not useful for promoting ethical behavior, and (3) that an empathetic person can lack other traits central to being virtuous, such as being motivated by the moral good and being disposed to do virtuous things whenever appropriate opportunity" (Simmons, 2014: 97). Like any moral property or theory, empathy will surely have objections against it. The literature on empathy, its role on morality, and its connection to altruism have proffered several responses to these objections. These scholars' major response, which we find attractive, insist that we need to work with what they refer to as "proper empathy", "morally countered empathy", and "fully developed empathic concern" (Carse, 2004: 169; Slote, 2005: 171, 2014: 97). Song (2014: 440) summarizes the literature that proposes proper empathy in this fashion: "Despite the differences in these accounts, they share a common idea, that it is not empathy *simpliciter*, but empathy in some proper form, that gives rise to correct moral judgment and action". Roughly, a proper empathy involves appreciating the epistemic and relational and caring components of it.

5 The book *Towards an African Political Philosophy of Needs*, among others, operates on the conception of human nature that is essentially characterized by need (Molefe & Allsobrook, 2021).

References

Barnes, M. (2014). Empathy. In: Teo, T. (Eds.), *Encyclopedia of Critical Psychology*. Springer, New York, NY.
Batson, C. D. (2012). The empathy-Altruism Hypothesis: Issues and Implications. In J. Decety (Ed.), *Empathy: From Bench to Bedside*. Cambridge, MA: MIT Press, 41–54.
Behrens, K. (2011). *African philosophy, thought and practice and their contribution to environmental ethics*. University of Johannesburg, Johannesburg.
Bujo, B. (2005). Differentiations in African Ethics. In W. Schweiker (Ed.), *The Blackwell Companion to Religious Ethics*. Malden, MA: Blackwell, 423–437.
Carse, A. (2005). The Moral Contours of Empathy. *Ethical Theory and Moral Practice International Forum* 8: 169–195.
Decety, J., & Jackson, P. L. (2004). The Functional Architecture of Human Empathy. *Behavioral Cognitive Neuroscience Reviews* 3: 71–100.
Decety, J. and Cowell, J. (2014). The complex relation between morality and empathy. *Trends Cognitive Science* 18: 337–339.
Democracy and Consensus in African Traditional Politics: A Plea for a non-Party Polity. *The Continental Review* 39: 53–64.
Dion, M. (1987). The Moral Status of Non-Human Beings and Their Ecosystems. *Ethics, Place & Environment* 3: 221–229.
Dzobo, N. (1992). Values in a Changing Society: Man, Ancestors, and God. In K. Wiredu & K. Gyekye (Eds.), *Person and Community: Ghanaian Philosophical Studies*, vol. I. Washington, DC: Council for Research in Values and Philosophy, 223–400.
Etieyibo, E. (2017). Ubuntu, Cosmopolitanism and Distribution of Natural Resources. *Philosophical Papers* 46: 139–162.
Gyekye, K. (1992). Person and Community in African Thought. In K. Wiredu & K. Gyekye (Eds.), *Person and Community: Ghanaian Philosophical Studies*, vol. I. Washington, DC: Council for Research in Values and Philosophy, 101–124.
Gyekye, K. (1997). *Tradition and Modernity: Philosophical Reflections on the African Experience*. New York: Oxford UP.
Hamilton, L. (2003). *The Political Philosophy of Needs*. Cambridge University Press.
Magesa, L. (1997). *African religion: the moral traditions of abundant life*. Orbis Books, New York.
Masolo, D. (2004). Western and African Communitarianism: A Comparison. In K. Wiredu, (Eds.), *Companion to African Philosophy* 483–498 Oxford: Blackwell Publishing.
Menkiti, I. (2004). On the normative conception of a person. In: Wiredu, K. (Ed.), *Companion to African philosophy*. Blackwell, Oxford, pp. 324–331.
Metz, T. (2007). Toward an African Moral Theory. *Journal of Political Philosophy* 15: 321–341.
Metz, T. (2010). Human Dignity, Capital Punishment and an African Moral Theory: Toward a New Philosophy of Human Rights. *Journal of Human Rights*, 9, 81–99.
Metz, T. (2011). Ubuntu as a moral theory and human rights in South Africa. *African Human Rights Law Journal* 11: 532–59.

Metz, T. (2012). An African theory of moral status: a relational alternative to individualism and holism. *Ethical Theory Moral Pract: Int Forum* 14: 387–402.
Molefe, M. (2015). A Rejection of Humanism in the African Moral Tradition. *Theoria* 63 (143): 59–77.
Molefe, M. and Allsobrook, C. (2021). *Towards an African Philosophy of Need*. New York: Palgrave Macmillan.
Molefe, M. (2020). *An African Ethics of Personhood and Bioethics*. Cham: Palgrave Macmillan.
Oruka, H. O. (1997). *Practical Philosophy: In Search of an Ethical Minimum*. Nairobi: East African Educational Publishers.
Pluhar, E. B. (1987). The Personhood View and the Argument from Marginal Cases. *Philosophica* 39: 23–38.
Ramose, M. (2009). The Death of Democracy and the Resurrection of Timocracy. *Journal of Moral Education* 39: 291–303.
Sherman, N. (1998). Empathy and Imagination. *Midwest Studies in Philosophy* 22: 82–119.
Simmons, A. (2014). In Defense of the Moral Significance of Empathy. *Ethical Theory and Moral Practice* 17: 97–111.
Singer, P. (2009). Speciesism and Moral Status. *Metaphilosophy* 40: 567–581.
Slote, M. (2005). The Dualism of the Ethical. *Philosophical issues* 15: 209–217.
Slote, M. (2007). *The Ethics of Care and Empathy*. New York: Routledge.
Slote, M. (2014). Virtue ethics and Sentimentalism. In Stan van Hooft & Nafsika Athanassoulis (Eds.), *Handbook of Virtue Ethics*. Acumen Publishing.
Snow, N. (2000). Empathy. *American Philosophical Quarterly* 37: 65–78.
Song, Y. (2015). How to Be a Proponent of Empathy. *Ethical Theory and Moral Practice* 18: 437–451.
Stueber, K. (2019). Empathy, The Stanford Encyclopedia of Philosophy (Fall 2019 Edition), Edward N. Zalta (Ed.), https://plato.stanford.edu/archives/fall2019/entries/empathy/.
Teffo, J. (2004). Democracy, Kingship, and Consensus: A South African Perspective. In K. Wiredu, (Ed.), *A Companion to African Philosophy*, 443–449. Malden: Blackwell.
Verhoef, H., Michel, C. (1997). Studying morality within the African context: a model of moral analysis and construction. *J Moral Educ* 26: 389–407.
Wamala, E. (2004). Government by Consensus: An Analysis of a Traditional Form of Democracy. In K. Wiredu, (Ed.), *A Companion to African Philosophy*, 435–442. Malden: Blackwell.
Wiredu, K. (1992). Moral Foundations of an African Culture. In K. Wiredu & K. Gyekye (Eds.), *Person and Community: Ghanaian Philosophical Studies*, vol. 1. Washington, DC: The Council for Research in Values and Philosophy, 192–206.
Wiredu, K. (1995). Democracy and Consensus in African Traditional Politics: A Plea for a Non-Party Polity. *The Centennial Review* 39: 53–64.

Part 2
African Applied Ethics

5 Ubuntu Ethics and Voluntary Euthanasia

Introduction

This chapter considers our obligations towards the dying in light of African ethics or Ubuntu thinking. The specific duty towards the dying we will consider relates to the bioethical question of the moral permissibility of euthanasia, specifically voluntary euthanasia. Roughly, *euthanasia* refers to a good death, a death meted out motivated by mercy towards the dying and suffering patient. Euthanasia is associated with mercy because it is usually recommended under extreme medical conditions, such as when a patient is terminally ill, with no prospect of a cure or recovery. The majority of literature on euthanasia tends to emerge from the Global North, and it is characterized by cultural, moral, and legal assumptions, particularly autonomy, salient in that context (Brock, 1993; Young, 2019). We evaluate the moral question of euthanasia from an African ethical standpoint. That is, we will use the axiological resources of Ubuntu thinking, specifically, the empathy-based account of value theory, to evaluate the place of euthanasia in African thought. We will argue that Ubuntu ethics permit voluntary euthanasia on three grounds, namely, (1) the teleological structure of Ubuntu thinking, (2) empathy-based considerations, and (3) preservation of dignity.

This chapter emerges motivated by the status of the literature in African philosophy concerning euthanasia. There is generally a scarcity of literature on euthanasia in African ethics (Mawere, 2009; Masaka, 2010; Maduka & Ojong, 2019; Metz, 2022). Moreover, this literature suffers from several concerning weaknesses in relation to engaging the theme of euthanasia. First, the approach tends to be anthropologically oriented rather than philosophical. Anthropological in the sense that it explores and endorses cultural practices in relation to euthanasia. For example, Fainos Mangena (2013: 127), a seasoned scholar of African philosophy, notes that "we are keen to determine if the concept of euthanasia is present in indigenous African thought". Our aim is a philosophical one, where, ultimately, we seek to identify a value and principle with an African pedigree and invoke it to determine the status, permissible or not, of euthanasia in African ethics.

Second, even the literature on African ethics that appears to be philosophical approaches this question in a way that is distinct from the approach we consider plausible. The common method of resolving bioethical issues involves the value or principle of human dignity. Note the comment, "Within applied ethics, the concept of dignity has been particularly salient in . . . bioethics. . . . It has also been invoked . . . in debates about end-of-life decisions and assisted euthanasia" (Bostrom, 2008: 175). Our aim is to contribute to debates on euthanasia considering an African-inspired account of moral status (or human dignity) to determine the permissibility of euthanasia. Hence, our work differs from those scholars of African thought who do not use the moral status approach to engage in these bioethical issues (Tangwa, 1996; Ramose, 1999; Masaka, 2010). For example, Masaka (2010) considers the situation of AIDS-related terminally ill persons under insufficient home-based care and argues that to reduce suffering, voluntary euthanasia is recommended. There is no appeal to an account of moral status, or human dignity, as the basis for this moral recommendation. There is reference to human dignity in the essay. This reference, however, is not in relation to it being the central concept to ground the choice for voluntary euthanasia. Moreover, the paper is not clear how it construes what, and which, among the various meanings of dignity, is central to euthanasia, supporting our reading that moral status (or human dignity) is not central in Masaka's approach.

The chapter proceeds as follows. The first section discusses the concept of moral status. In relation to this concept, we consider (a) its definition, (b) medical conditions usually associated with it, (c) types of euthanasia, and (d) methods of delivering it. The second section, using the parlance of "death with dignity", clarifies what notion(s) of "death" and "human dignity" are relevant in relation to the question of euthanasia. We specify "death as a process" as the relevant concept in discussions of euthanasia, and in relation to dignity, we identify achievement (or achievement) dignity as the relevant sense of dignity in debates on euthanasia without discounting intrinsic dignity. Finally, we justify euthanasia in relation to three considerations characteristic of Ubuntu thinking, specifically, teleology, empathy, and dignity. The teleological consideration perfectionist explains the metaphysical and moral condition under which euthanasia is justified, and empathy. The altruistic (care) triggered by empathy provides value-based considerations supporting euthanasia. The evasion of shame, unbearable pain, and suffering is consistent with protecting human dignity.

The Concept of Euthanasia

There are continuing debates concerning the most plausible characterization of euthanasia (Riisfeldt, 2023). Our aim does not involve defending the most plausible characterization of euthanasia; rather, we want to give the reader some understanding of it as a crucial concept in bioethics. We will specify an acceptable characterization of euthanasia so we can proceed to the goal of contributing an African perspective on the debates on euthanasia. Etymologically, the Greek word for *euthanasia* comprises two linguistic units – *eu* (good) and *thanan* (death) – which scholars tend to characterize to denote a good or merciful death (Koenane, 2017; Young, 2019). The death is described as good or merciful because it is typically expected that it will be administered in a way that is "easy" and "gentle" to facilitate "a painless death" (Gonsalves, 1985: 207).

The etymological analysis does capture the intuition that the death associated with euthanasia is distinct from other problematic instances of killing, such as murder, but it is not precise enough, in its own, to clearly distinguish it (Foot, 1977). The literature tends to specify two components as crucial in determining the character of euthanasia, which might distinguish it from other forms of killing, such as murder, namely, the *intention* to kill and the *purpose* motivating the killing (Foot, 1977; Riisfeldt, 2023). The death associated with euthanasia must be as a result of an intention to cause it. It is not a mistake. A medical practitioner intentionally kills the patient. The second component captures the purpose or underlying reason motivating the act of killing the patient. The medical practitioner kills the patient for the sole reason to benefit or relieve her from suffering. We can conceptualize euthanasia as involving a medical practitioner intentionally killing the patient to promote her good.

We need to clarify two things to make our definition more acceptable. First, under normal circumstances, the request must be issued from the patient. The patient must be able to make a request for euthanasia. Second, the good associated with euthanasia, as a good death, or the idea of the medical practitioner advancing the patient's good, makes sense when considered in the context of medical conditions usually associated with euthanasia. The literature usually associates the justifiability of euthanasia in the context of extreme medical conditions, which has been crystalized to the following five necessary conditions for the permissibility of euthanasia:

> a. is suffering from a terminal illness; b. is unlikely to benefit from the discovery of a cure for that illness during what remains of her life expectancy; c. is, as a direct result of the illness, either suffering intolerable pain or only has available a life that is unacceptably burdensome (e.g., because the illness has to be treated in ways that lead to her being unacceptably dependent on others or on technological means of life support); d. has an enduring, voluntary and competent wish to die (or has, prior to losing the competence to do so, expressed a wish to be assisted to die in the event that conditions (a)–(c) are satisfied); and e. is unable without assistance to end her life.
>
> (Young, 2019, n.p.)

We may consider the death associated with euthanasia to be good because it relieves the patient from excruciating pain, unbearable suffering, a burdensome and meaningless life, with no prospect of relief or a cure, or will not benefit from the cure. The consideration does take into account the modern sophisticated palliative capacities, but they are not always enough to address pain, and if they are enough, they leave the individual in such a drugged state that renders their lives meaningless or even pointless. Euthanasia has the potential to free or relieve the patient from the burden of pain and suffering, which conditions of existence render living meaningless, as it robs them of essential human functions and activities for no seeming purpose at all, at least from the perspective of suffering.

Types of Euthanasia

We can now proceed to distinguish the various types of euthanasia. If we consider extreme medical conditions usually associated with euthanasia, such as a person who is terminally ill but cognitively competent or an individual who is in a persistent vegetative state, where they are no longer conscious (hence, not cognitively competent), we can distinguish various types of euthanasia, namely, *voluntary*, *nonvoluntary*, and *involuntary* euthanasia. The major difference among the various types of euthanasia revolves around who makes the choice or requests for it. When a patient makes the choice, it is voluntary euthanasia. Often, the literature insists that the patient must have a sound mind and be cognitively competent and that the decision must be sustained or enduring (Brock, 1993; Young, 2019). When the patient loses their consciousness or cognitive competence due to terminal illness or is in a persistent vegetative state, a proxy may elect euthanasia on her behalf, which is nonvoluntary euthanasia. When a patient explicitly refuses euthanasia and the proxy, or the medical practitioner, or even the state, coerces it, we have involuntary euthanasia (ibid.).

In this chapter, we will limit our focus to the permissibility of voluntary and nonvoluntary euthanasia, considering Ubuntu thinking. Typically, in the Western tradition, two central values, or a principle holding these two values together, are invoked to justify the permissibility of euthanasia: "these values are individual self-determination or autonomy and individual well-being" (Brock, 1992). In relation to autonomy, the individual has a right to live life directed by their own conception of life, which extends also to questions of dying and how a person wants to die. Individuals must have control over not only how they live but also how they die. To be denied a right to be self-determining on questions relating to death is to violate a person's dignity. The value of well-being involves the question of the quality of life, whether one is better or worse off due to conditions related to being terminally ill. Brock (1992: 11) illuminates the well-being argument for euthanasia: "Others find the impairments and burdens in the last stage of their lives at some point sufficiently great to make life no longer worth living" and at this point prefer death to life. The conjoining of the values of self-determination and well-being "provide the moral foundation for requests for voluntary euthanasia" (Young, 2019: np). It is the value of the fundamental respect for human autonomy, which involves the right to choose how one ought to live her life or even die, and the value associated with conditions of living a life where one's quality of life is reasonable and acceptable. Should a patient's existence be at odds with these fundamental values, due to an irreversible and deteriorating terminal illness, whose state of existence is undignified, then voluntary euthanasia is permissible, which is the dominant argument from the West.

We will explore an argument that appeals to a different set of values, specifically, perfectionism, empathy, and the importance of preserving achievement (extrinsic dignity), which will offer an African and underexplored justification of voluntary euthanasia.

Methods of Euthanasia

The literature on euthanasia distinguishes between two ways to administer euthanasia, namely, passive and active euthanasia (Rachels, 1975). Passive euthanasia, sometimes described as indirect euthanasia, involves the medical practitioner withdrawing or withholding medical resources or assistance from the patient to allow her to die. Active, or direct, euthanasia involves a competent medical practitioner, using acceptable medical means, terminating the life of the patient. There is a debate in the literature on euthanasia concerning the validity of the distinction between passive and active euthanasia (Gerrard, 2005). On our part, we do not think this debate is relevant. The central question involves whether euthanasia itself is permissible; if it is, the question of how it will be administered will be secondary.

We turn to the question of death with dignity.

Death With Dignity

We will conceptualize our discussion and defence of the permissibility of euthanasia in relation to the idea of "death with dignity". We will start with the concept of death in the phrase "death with dignity", which we understand roughly to involve decent and humane conditions for the dying patient. African scholars distinguish between two distinct senses of death, the absolute and processual sense of death (Bujo, 2005; Molefe, 2022). "Absolute death" refers to the state of being entirely biologically nonfunctional, where the body, brain, and mind have ceased to be living organisms. "Process death" refers to the state where the agent is biologically deteriorating in the direction of absolute death, which may be relatively short or prolonged if there is no medical intervention or cure. Individuals in the final stages of aggressive cancer or HIV/AIDS may be described as experiencing processual death.

In an interesting essay, "Death with Dignity," Peter Allmark (2002) identifies four distinct concepts of death, namely, *nonbeing, transition, process,* and *the fact of mortality*. *Nonbeing* refers to the mystery associated with the fact of death. It is a mystery to us as subjects, or phenomenologically, we have no experiential content of being dead. The curtain between the phenomenology of being alive and being dead is insuperable, rendering death a perpetual mystery, psychologically speaking, for human beings. Death as transition seems to refer to the very final stages of the closing of one's life, the moment between being alive and being dead. Death as a process refers to the period designated as when we can suspect or have certainty that one is going to die, in our case, due to a medical condition. The moments associated with the individual's end of life. The fact of mortality does not require explanation; all of us cognitive competent human beings that hold reasonable beliefs know that one day we will die. It is a universal condition of sentient beings, death.

We might want to ask two related questions: Which concept of death is expressed in the phrase "death with dignity", and which concept of dignity is also expressed by this phrase? Remember that concerns associated with euthanasia revolve around the dying, that is, those that we suspect or have diagnosed to be living in the last moments of their existence, whose status and theme in bioethics is described as *end-of-life issues*. We believe that these considerations are sufficient to indicate that it is the sense of death, as a process, that is relevant in the context of euthanasia or death with dignity. In other words, when we invoke the idea of dignity in the context of the dying, we imagine them living and dying under conditions that recognize and affirm their dignity. Before we can make sense of conditions that recognize and affirm the dying patient's dignity, we need to be clear regarding the notion of dignity relevant in this context.

The literature in philosophy offers various meanings of the concept of human dignity. Michael Rosen (2012) distinguishes dignity as a status, intrinsic value, noble bearing of character, and as a right. Daniel Sulmasy (2008) distinguishes among intrinsic dignity, attributed dignity, and inflorescent dignity. Sarah Clarke Miller (2017) distinguishes between status and performance dignity, as does Michael (2014), except that he uses *status* and *achievement dignity*. For our purpose, it is the two senses of dignity that are relevant: status/intrinsic dignity and performance/inflorescent/achievement dignity. We consider status and intrinsic dignity to be equivalent expressions of the same basic idea that by merely being human, the agent, as a moral object, has value. Value traces the status of being human, or it is associated with the kind of thing a human being is. This is the kind of value associated with a human being that is not earned, conferred, and cannot be destroyed; in short, it is inalienable (Hughes, 2011). On the other hand, we have the equivalent expressions of dignity as something that comes about consequent to the agent's effort, and if the efforts were successful, then the s/he achieves dignity. This kind of dignity is conditional on the performance of the agent. It is a kind that one can lose relative to moral lapse or deterioration.

If the concept of death relevant to death with dignity is death as a process, it is not far-fetched to consider the most relevant concept of dignity in the talk of death with dignity to be achievement dignity. Two cases in the literature sustain this interpretation of matters. Allmark (2002), writing from a Western perspective, imagines conditions that might constitute a deviation from the ethos of death with dignity to be instances characterized by indignity in the context of dying. He understands an indignity to be an affront or insult to the patient's dignity. One instance of insult to the agent's dignity is when a medical practitioner lies or fails to disclose her diagnoses. In this view, if a good life or dignified life is a function of autonomous living characterized by the positive exercise of rationality and choice, then one's dignity is being insulted by being lied about their diagnosis. In the context of this example, death with dignity would require the agent to be told the truth about their condition so they can exercise their choices even in the context of dying.

Another case emerges in a non-Western context, the Confucian contribution to the literature of death with dignity. Note that some interpretations of Confucian moral thought recognize the distinction between status and achievement dignity, and the emphasis tends to be placed on the latter without discounting the former (Lo, 1999). This comment illuminates Confucian ethics in relation to death with dignity:

> Confucian ethics explicitly supports life-ending acts aimed at maintaining human dignity. For example, when an individual has to suffer humiliation as long as she lives and her dignity can only be kept by ending her life, death is righteous and worthy of pursuit. Similar cases include dying to achieve virtue or sacrificing one's life for justice.
>
> (Li & Li, 2017: 423)

Certain conditions of existence under achievement dignity, such as humiliation, should one suffering be characterized by conditions of humiliation, then euthanasia may be justified. One's biological deterioration may amount to physical and functional humiliation, which may justify voluntary euthanasia. Alternatively, in a context where there are no sufficient medical means to alleviate pain and suffering, voluntary euthanasia may be justified.

In this section, we have noted a discussion of death with dignity that considers conditions of existence that might undermine the dignity of dying patients; in this context, euthanasia may be justified. We considered examples from the Western and Chinese contexts. The section turns to Ubuntu thinking in relation to euthanasia.

Ubuntu and Euthanasia

To defend the permissibility of euthanasia in Ubuntu thinking, we perform the following tasks. First, we restate and refine our conception of Ubuntu ethics, where we conjoin the agent- and patient-centred aspects of it. We do this to highlight how intrinsic and extrinsic forms of dignity interact, which has implications that undermining one might have implications for another one also being violated. Second, we provide evidence from the literature in African philosophy that in African thought, we can meaningfully talk of death with dignity, or what we may consider a good death. Finally, we offer three moral-theoretical reasons grounded in Ubuntu thinking to justify euthanasia in African thought. We appeal to perfectionist, empathy-triggering altruism and achievement dignity in Ubuntu thinking to justify euthanasia.

Ubuntu Ethics, Final Good, and Dignity

In Chapters 3 and 4, we considered the final good and moral status and the relationship between them to account for African ethics, or Ubuntu thinking. In Chapter 3, the focus was on deriving a conception of moral status, or human dignity, from a conception of the final good in African ethics. Now, we spell more clearly how they function together to provide a robust interpretation of African ethics. We will do so by explaining the relationship between moral status and the final good in terms of human dignity. Remember, Ubuntu ethics prescribes the acquisition of *ubuntu* as the final good. We have also noted that *ubuntu* refers to a virtuous disposition, which is usually described in terms of being humane or caring. We have further refined and clarified *ubuntu* by interpreting it in terms of empathy. To have *ubuntu* amounts to having empathy. We have associated empathy with functions, which render it relevant in ethics, the epistemic and relational components, which play a crucial role to understand and connect with another person from their first personal and emotional perspective and to be supportive towards them. We have also endorsed the understanding of empathy that tethers it with altruism (or caring response). To have *ubuntu* amounts to being able to emotionally share and connect with another, empathy, and we note that empathy tends to induce altruism (or care).

We continued to argue, given the "ought implies can" principle, that we can derive an account of moral status (or human dignity) from the final good of *ubuntu*, or empathy. The "ought" part of the "ought implies can" principle refers to the final good, which involves the cultivation of empathy. The "can" part of the "ought implies can" principle refers to the intrinsic good, which we have associated with the metaphysical capacity for empathy (or *ubuntu*). Essentially, in our interpretation of Ubuntu thinking, human beings, by nature, are wired for empathy, and it is this essential and distinctive aspect of human nature that assigns them moral status, or human dignity. Hence, Ubuntu thinking, correctly construed, has at least these two crucial components, the capacity for empathy (moral status or human dignity) and the cultivation of empathy (to have *ubuntu*). The capacity for virtue embodies intrinsic value, and the cultivation of empathy embodies the final good. Human beings, as moral agents, can pursue *ubuntu* or cultivate empathy because they have the metaphysical capacity for it.

Now that we are clear about these two distinct components of value in African ethics, we can proceed to frame Ubuntu thinking in terms of human dignity. Remember, earlier, we noted the various meanings of human dignity. To express the interpretation of Ubuntu thinking in terms of human dignity, we will use Sulmasy's (2008) moral language and conceptual framework. Sulmasy distinguishes between *intrinsic* and *inflorescent* dignity. Intrinsic dignity refers to the value inherent in some entity, such as a human being, by virtue of the kind of thing that it is. It is some substantial feature of the kind, like rationality on the Kantian conception of human dignity, or, on our part, the capacity for empathy, which secures dignity. It is described as "intrinsic" because one has value merely for possessing the substantial features of the kind in which they belong, which features are value-endowing. Inflorescent (or achievement) dignity, according to Sulmasy (2008: 431), "refer[s] to individuals who are flourishing as human beings – living lives that are consistent with and expressive of the intrinsic dignity of the human". The recognition of the distinctive features that render one intrinsically valuable and their consistent development and exercise amounts to one flourishing as the kind of a thing she is. It is this kind of flourishing that develops our intrinsic features that count as achievement or inflorescent dignity. Note that in this sense of dignity, one flourishes relative to the habits and dispositions directly connected to those features that account for their intrinsic dignity, which involves habitually cultivating them.

Hence, on the one hand, we have intrinsic (or status) dignity because we have the capacity for empathy. On the other hand, we have inflorescent or achievement dignity because we have achieved *ubuntu* or have cultivated empathy. If we follow Menkiti's (1984) description of African ethics in terms of excellence, we can distinguish two kinds of excellences. There is the kind of excellence that attends to us merely for being the kinds of things that we are as human beings. There is also the kind of excellence that attends to our habits and dispositions as human beings. Although all human beings have the first kind of dignity, intrinsic dignity, or excellence, the second kind of dignity, achievement dignity, or excellence of character, is a function of the quality of the agent's actions and character. We will argue in the last section that inflorescent dignity can offer us a useful way to defend the permissibility of euthanasia.

The next section provides support for voluntary euthanasia.

Reasons Supporting Euthanasia

This section provides three reasons that Ubuntu thinking supports voluntariness. The reasons that we believe support euthanasia are associated with crucial features of Ubuntu thinking, namely, perfectionist/self-realization logic, dignifying empathy-based altruism (or care), and the preservation of achievement dignity.

Teleological Reason for Euthanasia

Ubuntu moral thinking has an essential teleological structure that defines the agent's moral purpose for existing – the perfection of character to have empathy. It is the agents' goal as long as they are alive to pursue moral growth. The goal of moral growth defines what counts as a meaningful and worthwhile existence. The very meaning or point of human existence involves cultivating empathy (and altruism or care) to create a humane world. The teleological structure of Ubuntu thinking plays the crucial role of defining the meaning, purpose, and goal of human existence. Human existence is meaningful if the agent can participate in morality, which involves the pursuit of perfection. The pursuit of perfection involves recognizing the source of our intrinsic value, or moral status, or human dignity, the capacity for virtue, which we must cultivate so we can flourish as beings of empathy (and care).

Following this reasoning, should an agent reach a point in their biological existence where this goal is impossible, under such conditions, voluntary euthanasia is justified. The reason for why euthanasia is justified involves the fact that their lives no longer have a purpose or meaning since they cannot participate in the great dance of personhood or perfection. Think of an individual who has leukaemia, in the final stages of it, and this person has lost all essential human functions; they are bed-bound, eat through the pipe, and cannot independently go to the toilet, and they live under heavy drugs and only have a short period in life before they die. There is nothing more that medicine and technology can offer them in terms of medical recovery or a cure, and they live under persistent and continually increasing pain and suffering. This condition has rendered them unable to participate in the goal of personal and moral growth. On the logic of the Ubuntu thinking, a patient in this condition may justifiably request euthanasia.

Note that the reason associated with the teleological structure is less subjective than the autonomy-based reason (Allmark, 2002). It is not the mere choice of the agent that is crucial; rather, it is the objective question of whether s/he can participate in the project of personal and moral development, which defines the purpose of her existence. On the mere fact that her life has turned entirely to be a burden to herself and possibly to those around her, with no meaning and hope, on the teleological reason, voluntary euthanasia may be granted. In this view, it is unjustified to request euthanasia when one can still recover or there is a cure. In fact, tough medical conditions can be an opportunity to learn, develop, and manifest courage in the face of medical adversity, which will contribute to one's personal growth – some circumstances, such as extreme but reversible medical conditions, are consistent with the project of cultivating virtue. Hence, reasons such as being tired of life or any such related kinds of considerations would not pass the test of permissibility. Ubuntu thinking restricts euthanasia based on lacking the capacity to participate in personal perfection, where there is no medical hope for relief or cure, which is no worse than other restrictions that one cannot simply request euthanasia because they are tired of life (Young, 2019). Personal choice has a place, so long as the agent has reached a point where they can no longer participate in morality.

There might be medical cases where the patient is extremely sick but they have not reached or may not reach the point where they can no longer participate in morality. On the teleological logic, medical practitioners and family members must urge the patient to be patient and to have courage, and they must also provide sufficient medical and family support, which is crucial on Ubuntu thinking, which tends to place a prime of positive and harmonious relationships. The objection that this trumps autonomy is moot because it begs the question by assuming that autonomy is the most important moral consideration. In African thought, autonomy is crucial, but it is framed ontologically and normatively in relational terms (Ikuenobe, 2015). It is in the context of engaging with various stakeholders, in the context of exploring medical options, opportunities, and resources, where decisions on the way forward may emerge – remember, I am because we are.

Empathy-Based Reason for Euthanasia

Ubuntu thinking, construed in terms of empathy, provides another reason to justify voluntary euthanasia. Remember, we associate empathy with the ability to read (understand) the inner experience of another person and to connect with them in a meaningful way that acknowledges their emotions and responds to them at their emotional level or perspective. We further noted that this kind of empathy tends to trigger altruism (or care). Empathy is a crucial epistemic and relational mode of being human that helps us recognize other human beings to affirm their humanity and humanize them through care (or altruism). The real debate in Ubuntu thinking involves appreciating the limits of empathy and care. To appreciate our argument, consider Enyimba and Ojong's (2019: 47) view for rejecting euthanasia based on Ubuntu thinking. They defend their view by arguing that "terminally ill persons are useful in the community in the sense that their condition provides the family members an opportunity to show how they care for them".

This reason for rejecting euthanasia strikes us as less than satisfactory. We find the framing of the terminally ill as "useful" as objects of care unfortunate and unnecessary. Terminally ill patients require care and support from their families and communities. We note that there are two related conditions that this interpretation of Ubuntu thinking overlooks or underestimates. First, we suggest that there is a point where our efforts medically and of care can no longer make any meaningful difference towards the terminally ill, where we can say "we have left it all in the hands of God". There is nothing we can do to address the need associated with health; our care is important but, at this point, meaningless because it makes no difference in terms of well-being.

Second, there is a point where the patient genuinely desires to be relieved from this endless, pointless, and persistent suffering and burdensome existence, where they can no longer participate in the very purpose of existence of moral perfection. We believe that empathy-based Ubuntu thinking would endorse empathy under such circumstances.

It strikes us as characteristically insensitive and bordering on cruelty to insist on prolonging a patient's life at a point where there is nothing we can do to reverse or ameliorate their situation, both physically and psychologically. At this point, at best, we can become spectators at the "spectacle" of human suffering until death prevails. Would altruistic care, in this instance, not permit euthanasia? This would surely not be an instance of properly empathizing with another in an extreme condition of need, where we can no longer meaningfully respond to their need. Worse, when the patient indicates the special need to be relieved from a burdensome existence of suffering through euthanasia, a truly empathetic response should consent to it. Empathy involves understanding another's need from their internal and personal standpoint; in this case, the patient requests to be relieved because their need for health can no longer be addressed by both medical and human comfort. Moreover, empathy involves (1) sharing (companying) something *meaningful* with the patient, the knowledge concerning her suffering and the genuine desire for relief through death; (2) *acknowledging* these feelings as important and mattering to the patient (rather than merely dismissing them); and (3) adjusting our response to speak to the need of the patient (rather than expressing what we feel, or think, is best). We believe that this kind of empathetic engagement would recommend voluntary euthanasia.

This kind of empathy could also be construed as dignifying (Miller, 2017). Empathy, in our view, induces care (or altruism), and it offers a distinctive way to express dignity with care (or altruism). Often, the most appropriate way to relate to beings of dignity involves the moral regard of respect, which is saliently characterized by constraints (i.e. not interfering or harming others). Moral regard to intrinsic dignity, where we understand dignity as the capacity for empathy, expresses the moral regard of respect from a different "register" than the one associated with Kantian ethics. Miller (2017: 114) captures it in this fashion: dignifying altruism (or care) "is an attitudinal recognition of another's dignity, but one that encourages the action of the carer stepping in to support the life plans of the one for whom they are caring". Dignifying care steps in to support, note, the life plan of the patient – it is the perspective of the patient of her own life that takes centre stage, and true care must be sensitive and responsive to it. Empathy is important because it facilitates proper understanding of the patient's life plans as important and mattering to her (epistemic dimension) and the kind of company, acknowledgement, and responsiveness (relational component), which is coupled by care (or altruism), that recognizes, affirms, and fulfils the patient's life plans, which, in this instance, ought to endorse voluntary euthanasia. If one of the manifestations of empathy involves being warm towards the suffering and relieving them of suffering, it would be plain insensitivity and even cruelty to simply ignore the desire of the patient to die peacefully.

Achievement Dignity and Euthanasia

We can also support voluntary euthanasia by appealing to the idea of inflorescent or achievement dignity. We do so given that the ideas associated with achieving *ubuntu* or personhood, which we have construed in terms of inflorescent or achievement dignity, can be associated with the idea of a good death, which offers a way to justify voluntary euthanasia. We articulate the idea of a good death in the background of inflorescent or achievement dignity. The idea of a good death can be gleaned in the debate on the normative idea of personhood or *ubuntu* between Menkiti and Gyekye in African thought. Gyekye (1992: 112–113) intimates the idea of a good death in this passage:

> Menkiti also argues that the relative absence of ritualized grief over the death of a child in African societies in contrast to the elaborate burial ceremony and ritualized grief in the event of the death of an older person also supports his point about the conferment by the community of personhood status. It is not true that every older person who dies in an African community is given elaborate burial. The type of burial and the nature and extent of grief expressed over the death of an older person depend on the community's assessment, not of his personhood as such, but of the dead person's achievements in life, his contribution to the welfare of the community, and the respect he commanded in the community. Older persons who may not satisfy such criteria may, in fact, be given simple and poor funerals and attenuated forms of grief expressions. As to the absence of ritualized grief on the death of a child, this has no connection whatsoever with the African view of personhood as such, as alleged by Menkiti.

The debate between Menkiti and Gyekye revolves around the correct understanding of personhood in African thought. Specifically, Gyekye is disputing that we can infer conclusions about the lack of personhood status of an infant relative to how it is buried. We believe that we can draw conclusions about the idea of a good death from this debate, specifically from the preceding passage. Gyekye draws a distinction between the death of an elder, an old person, and a child. In his view, it is not age per se that qualifies one for a great funeral. Rather, it is the achievements of the dead persons that secure them a great funeral. The funeral becomes an outlet to celebrate a successful and a worthwhile life. If you are old but were very useless, there will be nothing to celebrate. The reason a child is not generally offered an illustrious funeral is precisely because there is nothing to celebrate, because the child had not had an opportunity to achieve. The association of a good death with an elder is well calculated, and the longer one's life is, the more opportunity one has to achieve. Hence, the use of the elder is a paradigm case of a moral exemplar or a saint of the kinds of lives, and whose death, count as excellent, or a good one, which must be celebrated, celebrate a good life. The achievements associated with an elder are the kinds that endorse her intrinsic dignity and capacity for empathy; they amount to an inflorescent or achievement dignity.

The death of an elder, characterized by achievement dignity, or *ubuntu*, tends to be described as a good one. It is good in two ways. The agent has lived a long, productive, and excellent life characterized by success and achievement, that is, they made a positive contribution to humanity. Another sense that such a life is good is associated with *how* the agent dies. Tangwa (1996, 1995) expresses the second sense of the good death when he avers that when an "elder who has accomplished his or her mission in life falls sick, s/he would pray that, if her time has come, God take him/her speedily". Note, an elder who has accomplished her goals (i.e. she has inflorescent) prays for a speedy death. The reason for a speedy death might be that some forms of existence might be contrary to the inflorescent dignity and thereby undermine her intrinsic dignity. One such form of indignity finds expression due to pain and suffering, particularly one that cannot be relieved or where there is no chance of a cure. Tangwa (1996: 196) provides the reason that he supports voluntary euthanasia in this fashion:

"The view that pain and suffering are intrinsically bad probably comes as close as any to universal acceptance in both unreconstructed common-sense morality and in systematic normative morality." The Nso, in any case, certainly consider pain and suffering to be intrinsically bad.

It is the fear of suffering and pain that motivates the prayer and plea for speedy relief from the burdensome form of existence, wrapped in pain and suffering. An elder would not be considered to have had a good death, even after leading an illustrious life, should they be so defeated by old age and disease to a point where they become living objects of pain and suffering and are accompanied by the shame of the loss of control of essential human functions, where they slip into the zone of shame and indignity. If one dies peacefully before receding into a shameful condition of existence, coupled with their achievement dignity, we can rightly describe their death as a good one. Hence, we can conclude that the duty to preserve achievement dignity, particularly when there is evidence that medical care and human support cannot avail any good, all that is left is a life of shame (where one has lost essential human functions) and one wrapped in pain, supports voluntary euthanasia. Actions connected with achievement dignity are important because they are underlined by intrinsic dignity, and preserving the former recognizes and endorses the latter; hence, relieving someone through death before they slip into the zone of unjustified shame and suffering justifies voluntary euthanasia.

Conclusion

This chapter considered the bioethical question of euthanasia. We evaluated the question of the permissibility of voluntary euthanasia in light of Ubuntu thinking. We provided three reasons to justify euthanasia. The teleological structure of Ubuntu thinking provides an objective ground for when euthanasia is justified. When the patient has reached a point where they can no longer participate in the purpose of moral perfection, at this stage of their medical and biological deterioration, euthanasia is justified. At this stage, their existence can be described as burdensome, meaningless, and pointless since they can no longer fulfil their purpose. Empathy-based Ubuntu thinking, with its emphasis on altruism or care, offers another way to treat another, the patient in this instance, in a dignifying way. In this instance, empathy-induced care aims to be involved in the patient's life and support them in a way that is cognizant of their life plan, which also endorses voluntary euthanasia. Finally, a good death in Ubuntu thinking involves preserving and protecting achieved dignity from things such as unjustified suffering, shame, and total control of one's humanity, which stand out as glaring instances of indignity. This logic of avoiding unjustified shame and indignity, which is contrary to inflorescent dignity and threatens to reverse the achievements of the agent, recommends euthanasia.

The next chapter considers the moral status of dead bodies.

References

Allmark, P. (2002). Death with Dignity. *Journal of Medical Ethics* 28: 255–257.
Brock, D. W. (1992). Voluntary Active Euthanasia. *The Hastings Center Report* 22: 10–22.
Brock, D. (1993). Voluntary Active Euthanasia. *Hastings Center Report* 22: 10–22.
Bujo, B. (2005). Differentiations in African Ethics. In W. Schweiker (Ed.), *The Blackwell Companion to Religious Ethics*. Oxford: Blackwell Publishing, 419–434.
Enyimba, Maduka1, Ojong Lawrence O. (2019). A critique of euthanasia from the perspective of ubuntu (African) notion of mutual care. *International Journal of Advanced Scientific Research* 4: 47–52.
Foot, P. (1977). Euthanasia. *Philosophy and Public Affairs* 6: 85–112.
Garrard, E and Wilkinson S. (2005). Passive euthanasia. *Journal of Medical Ethics* 31: 64–68.
Gonsalves, M. A. (1985). *Fagothey's Right and Reason: Ethics in Theory and Practice*. St. Louis, MO: Times Mirror Mosby College Publishing.
Gyekye, K. (1992). Person and Community in Akan Thought. In K. Gyekye & K. Wiredu (Eds.), *Ghanaian Philosophical Thought Studies*, vol. 1. Washington, DC: Council for Research in Values and Philosophy, 101–122.
Hughes, G. (2011). The concept of dignity in the universal declaration of human rights. *J Relig Ethics* 39: 1–24.
Ikuenobe, P. (2015). Relational Autonomy, Personhood, and African Traditions. *Philosophy East & West* 65 (4): 1005–1029.

Koenane, J. (2017). Euthanasia in South Africa: Philosophical and Theological Considerations. *Verbum et Ecclesia* 38: 1–9.

Li, Y., & Li, J. (2017). Death with Dignity from the Confucian Perspective. *Theoretical Medicine and Bioethics*. DOI: 10.1007/s11017-016-9383-7.

Lo, P. (1999). Confucian Ethic of Death with Dignity and Its Contemporary Relevance. *The Annual of the Society of Christian Ethics* 19: 313–333.

Maduka, E. & Ojong, L. (2019). A Critique of Euthanasia from the Perspective of Ubuntu (African) notion of Mutual Care. *International Journal of Advanced Scientific Research* 5: 47–52.

Mangena, F. (2013). Euthanasia and the Experiences of the Shona People in Zimbabwe. *Thought and Practice: A Journal of the Philosophical Association of Kenya (PAK) New Series*, 5 (2), December 2013, pp. 123–136.

Masaka, D. (2010). A Theoretical Defense of Voluntary Euthanasia in the Context of AIDS Terminal Illness in Zimbabwe. *Journal of Sustainable Development in Africa* 5: 51–60.

Mawere, M. (2009). The Shona Conception of Euthanasia. *Journal of Pan African Studies*, 3 (4), December 2009, pp.101–116.

Menkiti, I. (1984). Person and Community in African Traditional Thought. In R. A. Wright (Ed.), *African Philosophy: An Introduction*. Lanham: University Press of America, 171–181.

Metz, T. (2021). *A Relational Moral Theory: African Ethics in and beyond the Continent*. Oxford: Oxford University Press.

Michael, L. (2014). Defining Dignity and Its Place in Human Rights. *The New Bioethics: A Multidisciplinary Journal of Biotechnology and the Body* 20: 12–34.

Miller, S. (2017). Reconsidering Dignity Relationally. *Ethics and Social Welfare* 11: 108–121.

Molefe, M. (2022). *Human Dignity in African Philosophy: A Very Short Introduction*. New York: Springer.

Rachels, J. (1975). Active and Passive Euthanasia. *New England Journal of Medicine* 292: 78–80.

Riisfeldt, T. (2023). Overcoming Conflicting Definitions of 'Euthanasia,' and of 'Assisted Suicide,' Through a Value-Neutral Taxonomy of 'End-of-Life' Practices. *Bioethical Inquiry* 20: 51–70.

Rosen, M. (2012). *Dignity: Its history and meaning*. Harvard University Press, Cambridge, MA.

Sulmasy, D. (2008). Dignity and Bioethics: History, Theory, and Selected Applications. In *The President's Council on Bioethics, Human Dignity and Bioethics: Essays Commissioned by the President's Council*. Washington, DC: President's Council on Bioethics, 469–501.

Tangwa, G. (1996). Bioethics: An African Perspective. *Bioethics* 10: 183–200.

Young, R. (2019). Voluntary Euthanasia. In E. N. Zalta (Ed.), *The Stanford Encyclopedia of Philosophy*. Retrieved October 30, 2019, from https://plato.stanford.edu/archives/fall2019/entries/euthanasia-voluntary/.

6 Ubuntu Ethics and the Moral Status of Dead Human Bodies

Introduction

This chapter considers the bioethical question of the moral status of dead bodies in Ubuntu thinking. The previous chapter considered the question of our duties towards the dying, specifically considering the place of voluntary euthanasia in Ubuntu thinking. The question that we now consider relates to the moral aftermath of the body when death has already occurred. That is, there are many philosophical questions that can be associated with death as a phenomenon, such as the metaphysical question concerning the afterlife (what happens to us when we die?), the question concerning the philosophical account of death itself (what is death?), the question of posthumous harm (can one be harmed posthumously?) (Feinberg, J. 1984; Metz & Molefe, 2021). These are important philosophical questions, but we limit our focus specifically to the dead human body, cadaver, or human remains (i.e. "material human remains per se") as an object of ethical inquiry (de Tienda & Currás, 2019). Our inquiry specifically involves ascertaining whether the dead human body, or cadaver, counts as a moral object, that is, whether it does have moral status, which would mean it is an object towards which we have direct moral obligations not to harm or to benefit.

In what follows, we clarify considerations regarding the importance of the question of the moral status of dead human bodies. First, there is a prevalent moral intuition among human cultures across the world that operates on the assumption that we owe dead bodies moral regard or respect (Rosen, 2012). This moral intuition in our cultures is displayed by the insistence of a decent or dignified funeral. We want to philosophically assess the plausibility of this moral intuition. Second, there are many ways to explore the question of the importance of dead bodies among human cultures. One possible, probably prominent, way might involve empirically surveying human cultures using cultural, historical, anthropological, psychological, or even archaeological tools to determine how human cultures have generally tended to relate to the human body. This kind of empirical work might give us interesting empirical facts or views concerning how cultures tend to view dead human bodies. We

DOI: 10.4324/9781032658490-8

need to clarify that ours is a philosophical project. We may consider some evidence from the empirical studies, and when we do so, we do so specifically to glean moral intuitions that are prevalent across different regions concerning the moral status of dead human bodies. For example, we note that a cursory survey of anthropological literature of the attitudes of African cultures towards dead bodies tends to hold them in high regard and demands that when we bury them, we should do so with dignity, which might be suggestive that they hold moral intuition or even the view that they do have moral status. At best, we consider such empirical data as intuitions that still require philosophical scrutiny before we can endorse or reject their plausibility (Matisson & Muade, 2022).

Third, another related way to consider this question might involve appeal to metaphysical or religious approaches. For example, African cultures operate with the metaphysical view of the afterlife. One such concerning manifestation of this belief relates to a now-jettisoned custom of the servants of a king; when he passes away, his servants would be killed, and the justification is that they will continue to serve the king in the afterlife (Wiredu, 1996). This metaphysical belief might have implications that for one to be able to proceed to the afterlife, they must have their body undamaged and whole. On this basis, one might assign moral value to the body. Another prominent metaphysical belief that might sponsor the value of the dead body is the belief in ancestors, an African concept that captures the afterlife (Menkiti, 1984; Metz & Molefe, 2021; Agada, 2022). One of the requirements associated with transitioning to join the spiritual community of ancestors involves the body being properly buried among loved ones. This metaphysical view might also have implications for the value of dead bodies.

Ours will be a strictly philosophical approach in relation to the question of dead bodies. We will follow the example of scholars who determine the moral status of dead human bodies based on moral status or human dignity (Metz, 2012; Molefe, 2017; Rosen, 2012). That is, the inquiry involves determining whether dead human bodies can count as moral patients, that is, things that morally matter for their own sakes or that have intrinsic value. Prominent moral intuitions and theories in moral philosophy would, for example, include normal adult human beings and animals, among others, in the moral community (Kittay, 2005; Nussbaum, 2009; Metz, 2012). Our question involves precisely considering whether we could or should extend moral citizenship and moral status to dead human bodies. Specifically, we will be considering whether dead human bodies do have moral status or whether the question of their death nullifies the once-normal and functional ontological capacities, which would exclude them from the moral community. In the final analysis, we will argue that Ubuntu thinking and influential moral theories both in the West and Africa regard dead human bodies as not having moral status.[1]

Finally, this project emerges because it might raise serious practical and bioethical implications. If it turns out that dead human bodies do have moral status, then it would seem many of our cultural practices might be correct. If, however, they do not have it, what are its practical implications? We will consider two practical cases in relation to the moral status of dead human bodies: (a) Are we justified in using dead bodies for scientific research of all kinds in archaeology, museums, and medical schools? (b) If dead bodies do not have moral status, how might we justify the intuition that we have some duties to regard dead bodies? In relation to (a), we will submit that we are justified in using dead bodies for scientific research. In relation to (b), we will argue that indirect moral consideration and autonomy might give us a ground to treat dead human bodies with respect.

We will structure the chapter as follows. The chapter is divided into three major sections. The first section revolves around theoretically scrutinizing the moral intuition that dead bodies do have moral status. To do so, it will first investigate influential secular moral theories that might imply regarding the moral status of dead bodies. It will consider two moral theories, Kantian ethics and Martha Nussbaum's capabilities approaches. Second, it will survey major moral theories of Ubuntu thinking, including the one being developed and justified in this book, the empathy-based approach, to consider their implications for the moral status of dead human bodies. In relation to both Western and Ubuntu thinking, it will emerge that both traditions of moral philosophy, including an empathy-based interpretation of Ubuntu thinking, entail that dead human bodies do not have moral status. We will take this conclusion as another way to validate the promise or plausibility of an empathy-based interpretation in that it does no worse than influential moral theories when reflecting on a controversial moral subject. Finally, we will consider the implications of the conclusion that dead bodies do not have moral status for (a) practical use of human remains, dead human bodies, in different contexts and (b) will try to justify our duties to treat dead bodies with respect by appealing to indirect considerations and autonomy.

Western Theories of Moral Status and the Moral Status of Dead Bodies

This section evaluates the moral status of dead human bodies considering Western moral theories. Space will not permit the survey of all Western theories. We will consider three moral theories, namely, Kantian ethics and capabilities approaches. At best, we offer a sketch of these philosophical views to assess their implications for our primary question.

Kant's Conception of Human Dignity

Immanuel Kant is probably the most influential modern philosopher. His contribution to the subject of human dignity philosophy is significant (Rosen, 2012). Roughly, on Kant's view, human beings have moral status, or human dignity, because they possess the capacity for autonomy, or rationality (Kant, 1996). Kant's view of human dignity, among others, emerges vividly in the second formula of humanity, which states, "Act in such a way that you treat humanity, whether in your own person or in the person of any other, never merely as a means to an end, but always at the same time as an end". The tendency in the literature is to understand the concept of "humanity" not to be a specific reference to a human being per se. Rather, "humanity" refers to the rationality nature or autonomy, whose features capture the inner, intrinsic, and absolute worth of the entities that possess such a property (Kant, 1996). According to Kant, "autonomy is . . . the ground of the dignity of human nature and of every rational nature" (1997: 43 [4:436]).

The call to treat humanity as an end may be roughly construed to be a call for moral agents to recognize "humanity" and respond accordingly towards it. If humanity has intrinsic and absolute worth, we should respond to it by expressing an attitude of respect, which Darwall (1977) captures as recognition respect. We understand *autonomy* to essentially refer to the human ability to frame (as a thinking being) one's life plan, to take responsibility and accountability to direct oneself according to a self-devised plan, and to recognize the good and rights of others (Wood, 2008: 54). To treat someone merely as a means involves treating them less than what their status of "humanity", (or rational nature) would demand, and it would amount to degrading and "dehumanizing" them into a status of a thing.

Considering this very rough sketch of the Kantian conception of human dignity, we may consider its implications for the moral status of dead human bodies. The moral status of a dead body will be determined by whether it does possess rational nature or not. It strikes us that the dead human body does not have a rational nature or autonomy, that is, it cannot direct itself towards certain goals of its own, take responsibility for them, and recognize others' rights. Hence, we cannot attribute moral status to it.

Nussbaum Capabilities Approach

Central to the capabilities approach is the fundamental value of freedom, or what Nussbaum (1988: 147) refers to as "substantial freedoms". Agents must have freedom to pursue valuable ends so they may live flourishing lives. The agent's freedom to be engaged in a variety of actions (doings) and to be (being whatever they want to be in the world) may be understood in terms of the distinction between *functionings* and *capabilities*. What people can do and be in the world refers to functionings. *Capabilities*, on the other hand, refer to the agent's opportunities to pursue functionings in the world. Nussbaum (2011: 20) describes capabilities to refer to "a set of . . . opportunities to choose and to act". She proceeds to observe that capabilities involve "alternative combinations of functionings that are feasible (for agents) to achieve" in the world (ibid.). She distinguishes between three kinds of capabilities, or real freedom, or opportunities, through which human agents can express or fulfil their lives, namely, basic capabilities, internal capabilities, and combined capabilities (Nussbaum, 2011). She describes the three distinct capabilities in this fashion:

> I use the term *basic capabilities* for the untrained capacities, the term *internal capabilities* for the trained capacities, and the term *combined capabilities* for the combination of trained capacities with suitable circumstances for their exercise.
>
> (2008: 357)

Basic capabilities refer to the raw equipment of our nature, such as the capacity for speech, writing, walking, and so on. Capacities are described as internal when the agent can actually use them because they have been developed or trained. Combined capabilities involve the interaction between internal and the sociocultural-political world. Combined capabilities give a picture, or way, to imagine real freedoms or opportunities of an agent in relation to her own personal development (internal capabilities) and the conditions in her world. If one wants to be a soccer player, his or her functioning might fail in two related ways. On the one hand, she may not achieve the physical development required for playing soccer. On the other hand, she may be able to play soccer (internal capability) but there are no opportunities to do so because there is a war or the place forbids women from playing sports. This view accounts for moral status, or human dignity, in relation to basic capabilities, which are necessary (though not sufficient) for functioning in the world. The mere possession of basic or raw human capabilities secures human dignity, a ground that explains the intrinsic worth of the entity and the respect we owe to it.

With this rough sketch, we may proceed to evaluate the moral status of dead human bodies. Dead human bodies lack moral status because they do not possess basic capabilities. They have no capacities that can be trained in pursuit of a flourishing life.

Next, we turn to various interpretations of Ubuntu thinking.

Ubuntu Thinking on Moral Status and the Dead

This section considers three interpretations of Ubuntu thinking to reflect on the question of the moral status of dead human bodies, namely, Metz's friendliness view, personality-based interpretations, and the empathy-based view.

Metz's Friendliness View

We provide a sketch of Metz's friendliness view with the assumption that the reader has already encountered it in Chapter 4. Metz defends a modal-relational view of Ubuntu thinking in relation to a conception of moral status. In this view, moral status is a function of the capacity for friendliness. Friendliness comprises two relationships, identity and solidarity. The former involves sharing a way of life within a group, where the agent conceives of her personal identity in terms of we rather than I; shares common goals with the group; and moreover, collaborates with the group to pursue the common goals. The latter, solidarity, involves goodwill, where the agent acts to promote the well-being or good of another for their own sake. The latter involves a caring, supportive, and empowering disposition towards others. Hence, friendliness involves sharing a way of life and being caring towards others.

Those entities that can both be subjects and objects of moral status have full moral status or human dignity. The paradigm case of full moral status, according to Metz, is normal adult human beings. It is the degree to which one can be a subject and object of friendly relations that determines full moral status. Hence, in this view, infants have moral status, but since they cannot be subjects of such relations, they lack full moral status or human dignity. Potentiality does not assign moral status on Metz's view; it is whether you can be a subject and/or object, and since infants can be objects of friendly relations, then they do have *some* moral status. Those that can only be objects of friendly relations, such as animals, in Metz's view, only have partial moral status. Two considerations qualify some entity to be an object of friendly relations. Matisson and Muade (2022: 72) rightly capture these two features for an entity to be an object of friendliness, and hence have partial moral status, as follows:

> According to Metz, for something to have partial moral status, it should have the capacity to benefit from subjects of friendly relations. That is, it should have the capacity for goal-directed behaviour, and its life should be such that it can be made better or worse off by friendly relations.

Given the rough sketch of Metz's account of moral status, we agree with observations in the literature that his account entails that dead human bodies lack moral status; they cannot be subjects of friendly relations, nor can they be objects of such relations – they lack self-directed behaviour, and they cannot be made better or worse off (Molefe, 2017; Muade & Matisson, 2022). Hence, dead bodies lack moral status.

Personhood-Based View of Moral Status

In Chapter 2, we encountered Menkiti's and Ikuenobe's personhood interpretation of moral status, or human dignity. We could refer to these as agential accounts of human dignity. On this account, moral status, or human dignity, is not a function of the mere possession of certain ontological capacities. The agential account of value completely denies the claim that human ontological capacities have intrinsic value. The agential accounts, at best, accord ontological capacities with only instrumental value. Instrumental value in as far as moral agents have the duty to perfect their capacities to realize the complete or "intrinsic" value, which is tantamount to achieving personhood. Without belabouring the point, on this interpretation of the personhood view of value, dead human bodies lack human dignity. The agential account of value locates two distinct ways one could have value, and the dead lack both. It assigns instrumental value in relation to the mere possession of certain ontological capacities – possession indicating the potential to use them, which is entailed by the very notion of instrumentality. It assigns human dignity only to those beings that have positively actualized their capacities to acquire excellence – the acquisition of excellence is tantamount to human dignity. The dead can no longer actualize their capacities and hence lack human dignity. In this view, we note that dead human bodies lack human dignity.

Empathy-Based Interpretation

The major difference between Ikuenobe's view and our interpretation of Ubuntu thinking is in relation to three points. First, we consider certain ontological capacities to have intrinsic value, which secures moral status, whereas his account denies this claim. Second, as much as we agree with Ikuenobe's view that the final good of Ubuntu thinking is the acquisition of personhood, normatively construed, or *ubuntu* (or being humane), we do not leave matters at merely associating these terms with virtue or excellence. We interpret personhood or *ubuntu* in terms of empathy, and we consider empathy to be the virtue that characterizes the essence of our humanity and the possibility of morality. When we say that some agent has *ubuntu*, we simply denote that she has empathy. In our view, empathy or *ubuntu* captures not the intrinsic good but the final good. Finally, we agree with Ikuenobe that *ubuntu*, as the final good, can be construed in terms of human dignity, but we do insist on the distinction between status/intrinsic and achievement/inflorescent dignity. Status dignity is a function of merely being human, characterized by certain substantial features of our nature. Achievement dignity refers to the dignity that emerges relative to the positive and successful instrumentalization/development of our capacities to embody *ubuntu* or to be characterized by an empathetic disposition. We believe Ikuenobe's view is wrong to locate foundational value on achievement dignity; rather, we consider status dignity as foundational in a correct interpretation of Ubuntu thinking (we have justified this view in Chapter 2). We have dignity because we have the capacity for virtue, and the development of this capacity amounts to the acquisition of *ubuntu* (or an empathetic disposition).

If on the empathy-based view we have moral status because we have the capacity for empathy, anything that lacks this capacity does not have it. The conclusion is unavoidable that dead human bodies lack this capacity. Hence, on the empathy-based view, dead human bodies lack moral status.

In sum, the previous two sections surveyed a sample of influential moral theories both in the Western and African moral traditions. Theories in the West specify the capacity for autonomy and basic capabilities to account for moral status, or human dignity. Ubuntu thinking variously prescribes, depending on the moral theorist, the capacity for friendliness, the agential account of value, and the capacity for empathy. All these theories, from the West and Africa, lead to the conclusion that dead human bodies lack moral status. Being dead has such a massive metaphysical implication for the dead body that it can no longer be party to concerns of morality in the way a living human being is. It is the potential that ontological capacities must affect a living human being in the context of interacting with other human beings (and sentient beings) where they are relevant. In the context of death, ontological capacities cannot be affected either positively (think here of development and/or positive use of capacities) or negatively (think here of harm that degrades and undermines the possessor of capacities), morally or even nonmorally.

On our part, we consider the implications of the empathy-based account of moral status in the company of other moral theories' implications for dead human bodies because we believe that this could provide us with a vantage point to evaluate its promise or plausibility as a moral theory. We say so because we believe that there are at least two ways a moral theory can be plausible. On the one hand, a moral theory can differ from prominent theories in terms of the conclusion they reach in relation to a particular theme. The theory will count as plausible if it can provide a compelling or stronger rationale or account than extant prominent theories. On the other hand, a theory can be considered plausible in the event that, in relation to a particular theme, it does no worse than its competitors. In other words, we would have considered an empathy-based interpretation of Ubuntu thinking a weak instance of it had it differed from the dominant view in the literature that dead human bodies lack moral status, but it failed to provide compelling reasons to justify this view. This option did not emerge in relation to an empathy-based account. On the other hand, the fact that it reaches a similar conclusion as competing moral theories both in Africa and the West provides further prima facie reasons that it embodies moral-theoretical promise as a moral theory with an African pedigree.

The conclusion that an empathy-based account does no worse than its competitors should be taken very seriously. It reveals something about the assumptions and structures of our moral theories. Our moral theories paradigmatically construe morality, in one way or another, in terms of some essential (human) capacity and the functions associated with it. These theories characteristically imagine moral patients and moral agents as their objects, at the very least sentient beings. Hence, the structure of both African and Western moral theories imagines sentient beings possessing certain essential ontological features as crucial inputs in framing morality. Hence, we observe that the empathy-based approach embodies this paradigmatic feature of moral theories.

Ubuntu Ethics and the Moral Status of Dead Human Bodies 105

The next section turns to the practical implications related to the moral status of dead human bodies.

Practical Implications

This section has two tasks. The first task considers the question of whether it is permissible to use dead human bodies for scientific endeavours. The second task involves expounding indirect considerations that might offer other grounds to secure the prevalent moral intuition that we ought to treat dead human bodies with respect and/or dignity.

The Justifiability of Using Dead Bodies in Scientific Research and Practice

The use of dead human bodies, or human remains, is featured in certain scientific disciplines and often leads to moral concerns. In archaeology, the question of moral status can be posed in this fashion: Is there something "wrong with moving, analysing, and exhibiting an inert body"? (de Tienda Palop, 2019: 19). The purpose of digging, moving, analyzing, and exhibiting an inert body in archaeology is to contribute to understanding human history, civilizations, and ancient cultures, among others. Museums also keep or display human remains for academic and research purposes. Consider the controversial case (as an example of a medical museum) of the Cushing Center at the Yale School of Medicine. This centre exhibits collections of human brains to display certain brain pathological features. It accompanies the human brains kept in a see-through container with the picture and name of the patient (Sallam, 2019). Consider also the case of the use of human remains for teaching, learning, and scientific investigations in medical schools. One commentator remarks as follows in relation to the use of unclaimed cadavers in the context of America: "Use of unclaimed bodies for anatomy teaching in undergraduate medical education continues, but is ethically controversial" (Caplan & DeCamp, 2019: 360). Another research group notes, "The panellists agreed about the importance of using cadaveric material to teach anatomy, but the provision, sources and procedures are followed to get them from one to another country and/or university".

In relation to the use of human remains, whether in archaeology, museums, medicine, or any related discipline, our moral contribution in relation to the question of the moral status of dead human bodies is that they do not have moral status. In other words, and in principle, the principle we invoke here is a *moral* one based on the idea of moral status, which informs the view that the use of human remains in archaeological, anthropological, historical, and medical research is permissible. That is, if there are only two deciding considerations, namely, the method of moral status and the dead human body itself detached from other (cultural) factors, it is permissible to use them for such scientific pursuits, among others. The basic claim is that the body itself as it is, when it is dead, is not an object of moral concern. We are aware that matters when it relates to dead bodies are complex that the two considerations we have just suggested. There are questions related to questions of loved ones, whether we are dealing with the remembered (the dead bodies that can still be associated with living human beings and relatives) or the forgotten (the dead bodies that cannot be directly connected with any human beings, for example, thirteenth-century graves in some undiscovered land) dead, the questions of cultures and rituals associated with human remains, and so on.

It is our view that strictly, morally speaking, informed by considerations related to the evidence adduced in terms of moral status, dead human bodies have no moral status. It is not our conclusion, however, that there are no other grounds to consider the ethical use of human remains (though we consider the question of moral status to be a primary moral consideration). In other words, as much as the dead body has no moral status, there might be other ethical considerations that may limit acts that we may do towards them. Next, we consider such considerations.

Indirect Moral Considerations

As much as we have established that dead human bodies have no moral status, we want to suggest that there might still be secondary ethical considerations to justify many of our cultural practices aimed at respecting dead human bodies. The respect we are invoking is not the deep one that resonates with intrinsic value, recognition dignity. It is a lighter version of respect as some kind of moral regard. To clarify how we can still justify many of our practices of respecting dead bodies, we will invoke two kinds of ethical considerations, the indirect defence of securing our duties towards dead human bodies and considerations associated with the moral concept of autonomy.

The distinction between direct and indirect obligations gives us a clue of an important ethical consideration to protect and respect dead human bodies. We have direct duties towards things that have moral status, that is, these duties arise in relation to and for the entity that has moral status (DeGrazia, 2013). Indirect duties arise in relation to protecting the interests or good of the entity that has moral status via not harming or interfering with a thing that in and of itself does not invite moral consideration that has a connection with the former. Think of the relation between the chair owner and the chair. We have a duty not to steal or break the chair. Our duty, ultimately, not to steal or break the chair is towards the owner of the chair and not the chair itself. The duty that we have towards the chair is indirect. Had the chair been without an owner, then we could do with it as we please; whether we steal or break it would not occasion any moral concerns. This kind of strategy has been invoked in a variety of contexts to protect certain important human interests and other nonmoral objects, such as the environment and animals. Consider the case of animals in Kant's moral philosophy as an instance of this kind of indirect defence of animals.

On Kant's view, at least as we interpret it here, only those entities bearing rational nature (or autonomy) have moral status or human dignity. One implication of this view is that animals do not have moral status because they lack a rational nature. Note Kant's (1997: 212) indirect argument for protecting animals:

> If a man shoots his dog because the animal is no longer capable of service, he does not fail in his duty to the dog, for the dog cannot judge, but his act is inhuman and damages in himself that humanity which it is his duty to show towards mankind. If he is not to stifle his human feelings, he must practice kindness towards animals, for he who is cruel to animals becomes hard also in his dealings with men.

We do not have a duty towards the dog because it lacks the relevant moral ground of rational nature. Because the dog lacks the rational nature, in and of itself, it does not occasion moral issues. The act of killing the useless dog, however, should not be done because it poses a moral threat to humanity and the morality of the human agent. By killing the dog, the man would be debilitating the sensitivity towards sentient beings and strengthening propensities of cruelty towards them, which may extend towards fellow human beings. To protect the quality of our humanity in terms of our nurturing and protecting sensitive, kind, and responsive dispositions, we should extend some considerations of kindness towards animals for own sakes, which ultimately does offer some kind of protection for animals.

We believe that indirect defence of dead human bodies might be sufficient to accommodate many of our practices of respect towards them (dead human bodies). We must not act in inhumane and cruel ways towards dead human bodies, because that might strengthen our disposition to be cruel and unkind to fellow human beings. This consideration at an individual and cultural level is important in fostering empathetic and altruistic attitudes towards our treatment of dead bodies as the affirmation that they are a part of the human community and that we will also go through the same route of being dead bodies. This kind of indirect defence is at home in Ubuntu thinking. Remember, Ubuntu urges the moral agent to pursue *ubuntu* (or empathy). If being insensitive towards dead human bodies is antithetical to the goal of empathy, it would follow that we would have to adopt cultural means of relating to dead bodies that do not denigrate our humanity and the prospects associated with the goal of moral perfection. The indirect defence should be enough to justify many of our cultural practices of protecting and respecting dead bodies. These practices, however, should be properly construed as ultimately resting on indirect consideration either to protect our project of acquiring *ubuntu* or expressing the desire to be treated in humane ways when we also die and not wrongly to suggest that dead bodies do have moral status.

Even though the dead body has no moral status, the validity of this claim does not render the moral consideration associated with autonomy irrelevant in dealing with them (dead bodies). Instead, autonomy provides an important ground to account for the respect of dead bodies. If, for example, an individual or a particular culture refuses to be cremated as a form of disposing of human remains, it would be immoral to do so should one, without any justification, simply cremate the human remains of this individual or members of this cultural group. The autonomy of the now-dead person, or the family, as the proxy, or the cultural group, should count for something in relation to how the body should be disposed. On this consideration, it would be immoral for a scientist to steal bodies to do research, no matter how great the consequences of the scientific endeavour. It is not that autonomy is a trump card; it should be a cardinal feature of robust ethical cultures, particularly when it is construed in ways that affirm the sociocentric rather than egocentric approach, or what scholars term *relational autonomy* (Molefe, 2020). Although the act of stealing would not harm the dead body itself, in the sense of undermining its intrinsic value, it will undermine other important moral considerations relating to autonomy (or even legal issues of criminality). Hence, the case of the use of unclaimed cadavers in medical schools for training in anatomy and physiology is not ethically objectionable at a fundamental moral level, where the only moral considerations are related to the question of moral status. Ethical objections and controversies emerge, however, when we invoke the indirect moral consideration or the moral consideration of autonomy in relation to claimed cadavers.

Conclusion

This chapter considered the question of the moral status of dead human bodies in light of Ubuntu thinking, specifically, the empathy-based account of moral status. The chapter began by sampling prominent moral theories in both Western and African contexts to assess the standing of dead human bodies. It concluded that prominent moral theories do not assign moral status to dead human bodies. Moreover, it argued that if the empathy-based account of moral status also entails the same conclusion as other prominent and emerging theories, then it is reasonable to consider it to warrant it being taken seriously. We also considered two important practical questions in light of our conclusion regarding dead human bodies lacking moral status. First, we noted that dead bodies having no moral status implies that it is permissible to use them for scientific reasons in disciplines such as archaeology and medicine, among others. Second, we adduced the indirect defence argument and the value of autonomy to defend many of our cultural practices aimed at showing regard towards dead bodies. Failure to regard dead bodies might undermine our project of acquiring *ubuntu* (or empathy). Moreover, the value of autonomy might also require that we consider the wishes of dead human beings, family, and cultures with regard to dead bodies.

Note

1 We are aware that Matisonn and Muade (2022) did pursue the question exploring the moral status of dead bodies in African thought. Their paper animated from Muade's (2020) doctoral thesis, which had been supervised by Mattison. Our project differs from theirs in several crucial ways. First, our purpose is to explore and justify the plausibility of Ubuntu thinking, which was not their purpose. Their purpose is the question of the moral status of dead human bodies. They consider both a very limited sample of secular and religious theories of moral status; we limit ourselves strictly to secular interpretations of Ubuntu thinking. We will try to expand the sample to strengthen our conclusion that dead bodies do have moral status.

References

Agada, A. (2022). Shifting Perspectives in African Philosophy of Religion. *Religious Studies* 59: 291–293.

Caplan, I., & DeCamp, M. (2019). Of Discomfort and Disagreement: Unclaimed Bodies in Anatomy Laboratories at United States Medical Schools. *Anatomy Science Education* 12: 360–369.

Darwall, S. (1977). Two Kinds of Respect. *Ethics* 88: 36–49.

DeGrazia, D. (2013). Equal Consideration and Unequal Moral Status. *The Southern Journal of Philosophy* 31: 17–31.

de Tienda Palop, L., & Currás, B. X. (2019). The Dignity of the Dead: Ethical Reflections on the Archaeology of Human Remains. In K. Squires, D. Errickson, & N. Márquez-Grant (Eds.), *Ethical Approaches to Human Remains*. Cham: Springer, 19–37.

Feinberg, J. (1984). *Harm to Others: The Moral Limits of the Criminal Law*. Oxford: Oxford University Press.

Kant, I. (1996). *The Metaphysics of Morals*. Translated by M. Gregor. Cambridge: Cambridge University Press.

Kant, I. (1997). *Groundwork of the Metaphysics of Morals*. Translated by M. Gregor. Cambridge: Cambridge University Press.

Kittay, E. (2005). Equality, dignity and disability. In: Waldron, A., Lyons, F. (Eds.), *Perspectives on equality: the second Seamus Heaney lectures*. Liffey, Dublin, 95–122.

Luper, S. (2021). Death. In E. N. Zalta (Ed.), *The Stanford Encyclopedia of Philosophy*. https://plato.stanford.edu/archives/fall2021/entries/death/ (accessed 20 May 2023).

Matisonn, H., & Muade, N. E. (2022). Research on Dead Human Bodies: African Perspectives on Moral Status. *Developing World Bioethics* 23: 67–75.

Matisonn, H., & Muade, N. E. (2023). Research on Dead Human Bodies: African Perspectives on Moral Status. *Developing World Bioethics* 23: 67–75.

Menkiti, I. (1984). Person and Community in African Traditional Thought. In R. A. Wright (Ed.), *African Philosophy: An Introduction*. Lanham: University Press of America, 171–181.

Metz, T. (2012). An African Theory of Moral Status: A Relational Alternative to Individualism and Holism. *Ethical Theory and Moral Practice: An International Forum* 14: 387–402.

Metz, T., & Molefe, M. (2021). Traditional African Religion as a Neglected Form of Monotheism. *The Monist* 104: 393–409.

Molefe, M. (2017). A Critique of Thad Metz's African Theory of Moral Status. *South African Journal of Philosophy* 36: 195–205.

Molefe, M. (2020). *An African Ethics of Personhood and Bioethics: A Reflection on Abortion and Euthanasia*. New York: Palgrave Macmillan.

Muade, E. (2021). Towards a Theory of Moral Status of the Dead and its Contribution to Medical Research and Learning: The Case of Unclaimed Cadavers. [Dissertation]. Pietermaritzburg: UKZN.

Nussbaum, M. (1988). Nature, Functioning and Capability: Aristotle on Political Distribution. *Oxford Studies in Ancient Philosophy* (Supplementary Volume) 6: 145–184.

Nussbaum, M. (2009). The Capabilities of People with Cognitive Disabilities. *Metaphilosophy* 40: 331–351.

Nussbaum, M. (2011). *Creating Capabilities*. Cambridge, MA: Harvard University Press.

Rosen, M. (2012). *Dignity: Its History and Meaning*. Cambridge, MA: Harvard University Press.

Sallam, A. (2019). The Ethics of Using Human Remains in Medical Exhibitions: A Case Study of the Cushing Center. *Yale Journal Biology and Medicine* 92: 765–769.

Wiredu, K. (1996). Reply to English/Hamme. *Journal of Social Philosophy* 27: 234–243.

Wood, A. (2008). Human Dignity, Right and the Realm of Ends. *Acta Juridica* 1: 47–65.

Index

abortion 5, 20
achievement dignity 86–89, 103; and euthanasia 93–94
Africa 7, 13n6, 29, 65, 68, 98, 104; as term 9–11
African analytical philosophy 11–12
African communitarianism 48
African ethical theory 3–5, 18, 59–60
African ethics 3–13, 13n5, 18, 29, 41, 45–47, 49–50, 53–55, 56n4, 59–60, 63, 65, 67, 69–70, 75, 76n1, 81–82, 88–89
African moral philosophy 3–4, 13
African moral thought 3–4, 29, 42, 46–47, 51, 64–65, 68–69, 72
African philosophy 3–6, 8–9, 11–13, 13n4, 13n6, 14n7, 42, 54, 68, 81, 88; moral status in 18–38
African socialism 47
Afro-communitarianism 47–48
afterlife 97–98
agency 28, 55; moral 74; rational 21
AIDS 82, 85
Akans 55, 65, 68
altruism 42, 47–54, 56, 56n3, 60–63, 66–67, 76n4, 88, 90–92, 95, 107; empathy-based 42, 67, 71, 82, 88–89; practical 48; *ubuntu* as 47–51; *see also* empathy-altruism hypothesis
AMC 71–73, 76
analytical philosophy: African 11–12
analytic philosophy 11–12, 14n7
ancestors, spiritual community of 98
animal ethics 5, 33
animals 22, 31, 33, 36, 37n1, 60, 70–76, 98, 102, 106–107; *see also* animal ethics

applied ethics 82; and problem of death 8
autonomy 8, 21, 28, 81, 84–85, 90–91, 99, 100, 104, 106–108; relational 65, 108

Bantu people 7
behaviours 29, 42, 45, 47; altruistic (caring) 60; goal-directed 102; pro-social 44–45, 53, 61, 63; self-directed 102
bioethical issues 7, 82
bioethics 4, 7–8, 82–86; African 8; *see also* bioethical issues
Black people 37

cadavers 4, 8, 97, 105, 108; *see also* dead human bodies
capabilities 8, 21, 22, 25, 100–101; basic 21, 101, 104; combined 101; internal 101; *see also* capabilities approach; cognitive capabilities approach 21–22, 99–101
cognitive 61; abilities 20, 21, 72; attributes 21; competence 84, 86
common good 50, 63; and empathy 67–69
communitarian ethics 27, 47–48
communitarianism 48, 67; African 48; Afro- 47–48
Confucian ethics 87
Confucian moral thought 87
consensus 10, 63, 76; and empathy 67–69
contractualism 22

dead bodies 8, 97–108; friendliness view 101–102; indirect moral

considerations 106–108; moral obligations toward 8; moral standing of 4; moral status of 8, 95, 97, 99–101, 109n1; in scientific research and practice 105–106; Ubuntu thinking on 101–105; *see also* capabilities approach; dead human bodies; Kantianism
dead human bodies: moral standing/status of 4, 8, 13, 97–108, 109n1; unclaimed 105, 108
death 3–13, 40, 82–88, 92–95, 97–98, 104; absolute 85; African ethics and 8; applied ethics and the problem of 8; with dignity 82, 85–88; good 8, 81, 83, 88, 93–95; merciful 83; problem of 4–5, 8; process 85
dignity 85–89, 92–95; attributed 86; death with 82, 85–88; extrinsic 85, 87; factual 28–29; inflorescent 86, 89, 93–95, 103; intrinsic 74, 82, 86–87, 89, 92, 94; Kantian conception of 89, 100; performance 86; status 86–87, 103; *see also* achievement dignity; human dignity

egalitarianism 18; moral 29, 33–35
egoism 49–51
empathy 7–8, 12–13, 40–42, 44, 51, 54, 56, 56n3, 59–76, 76n1, 76n2, 76n3, 76n4, 81–82, 85, 88–93, 95, 99, 101, 103–104, 107–108; -based altruism 42, 67, 71, 82, 88–89; and common good 67–69; and consensus 67–69; as defining essence of Ubuntu ethics 63–69; definition 60–63; developed 42, 51–54, 56, 61–63; proper 61–63, 76n4; vs friendliness 69–75; human need and 65–67; human relationality and 64–65; morally countered 76n4; *ubuntu* as 51–54; *see also* empathy–altruism hypothesis
empathy–altruism hypothesis 42, 52–53, 61–63
end-of-life decisions 82
end-of-life issues 4, 86
environmental ethics 5

ethical humanism 6, 65
ethical monism 13n1
ethical naturalism 6, 13n4, 20
ethical pluralism 13n1
ethical supernaturalism 6, 20
ethical theory(ies) 27, 52; African 3–5, 18, 59–59
ethics 3, 6–7, 20, 22, 25, 27, 29, 37, 46, 52, 65, 68, 88; African 3–13, 13n5, 18, 29, 41, 45–47, 49–50, 53–55, 56n4, 59–60, 63, 65, 67, 69–70, 75, 76n1, 81–82, 88–89; animal 5, 33; applied 8, 82; care 21, 65; communitarian 27, 47–48; Confucian 87; environmental 5; feminist 65; Kantian 92, 99–100; meta- 52; normative 52; *see also* bioethics; Ubuntu ethics
European moral philosophy 49
euthanasia 4, 8, 13, 76; achievement dignity and 93–94; active/direct 85; concept of 82–85; empathy-based reason for 91–93; involuntary 84; methods of 85; nonvoluntary 84; passive/indirect 85; reasons supporting 89–94; teleological reason for 90–91; types of 84–85; Ubuntu ethics and 81–95; voluntary 81–82, 84–85, 87, 89–95, 97

final good 7, 40–42, 55–56, 56n1, 56n4, 88–89, 103; general account 42–47; *ubuntu* as altruism 47–51; *ubuntu* as empathy 51–54
foundationalist approach 35–36
friendliness 6–7, 42, 46–47, 59–60, 76, 101–102, 104; vs empathy 69–75; *see also* friendliness theory
friendliness theory 59
"full moral status" (FMS) 3, 22–23, 24–25, 70–71, 73, 102
functionings 100

German philosophy 7
Global North 81
God 12, 28, 91, 94
good death 8, 81, 83, 88, 93–95; *see also* euthanasia

human dignity 3–4, 7, 13n2, 19, 22–25,
    28–30, 34–37, 37n1, 43,
    56, 56n4, 70, 82, 86–90, 98,
    101–104, 107; and excellence
    103; Kant's conception of
    99–100; in modern politics
    35–37; *see also* dignity
humaneness 41–42, 44–48, 50–51,
    53–54, 56n3, 85, 88, 90, 103,
    107
humanism 13n4; critical 47; ethical 6, 65
human minimum 66
human nature 6, 13n4, 28, 36–37, 44, 46,
    64–65, 67, 69, 77n5, 88, 100
human needs 65–67; moral 65–66; well-
    being 65–66; *see also* human
    minimum
human remains 4, 97, 99, 105–106, 108;
    see also dead human bodies
human rights 18, 27, 29; in modern
    politics 35–37
Hume, David 52
Hutcheson 52

"I am because we are" 46, 64, 91
identity 70, 102
imago dei 20
individualist(ic) approaches 21–22, 25
instrumentality 103
intrinsic good 41, 70, 88, 103
intrinsic value 4, 20–21, 27–32, 35,
    36, 43, 74–75, 86, 88, 90, 98,
    102–103, 106, 108

Kant, Immanuel 21, 99–100, 107
Kantian ethics 92, 99
Kantianism 21–22, 99–100; and human
    dignity 89, 99–100
Kaunda, Kenneth 47

life 6, 8, 10, 28–29, 33, 44, 48, 50, 56n4,
    62, 66–68, 70, 83–87, 90–95,
    100–102; good 28, 87, 94;
    human 48, 66; quality of 10, 33,
    56n4, 84–85; *see also* afterlife;
    death; end-of-life decisions;
    end-of-life issues
living human beings 104, 106; as proper
    objects of morality 8

maximalism 27, 32, 35
mercy killing 8; *see also* euthanasia

merit 25, 28–29, 31, 33, 36
Metz, Thaddeus 8, 10, 12, 22, 45, 49,
    51, 56n4, 59–60, 67, 69–74,
    101–102; *see also* friendliness
    theory
minimalism 26–27
moral agency 74
moral agents 3, 19–20, 26, 28, 32, 35,
    40–41, 43, 46, 56, 61, 68, 88,
    100, 103–104, 107
moral communities 18, 32–33, 98
moral culpability 26
moral egalitarianism 29, 33–35
moral equality 33
moral evil 33
moral goal 7, 43
moral holism 71, 73–75
moral individualism and relationalism
    19, 21–22
moral intuition 8, 32, 52, 67, 76, 97–99,
    105
morality 6, 8, 13n4, 19–21, 26–27,
    29, 31, 37, 40–41, 44–45, 48,
    52–53, 55–56, 60–62, 65–68,
    74, 76n2, 76n4, 90–91, 94,
    103–104, 107; action-centred
    55; agent-centred 55
moral judgment 76n4
moral liability 26
moral logic 49
moral object 18, 62, 86, 97; non- 106
moral obligations 3, 8, 18, 21, 25, 52, 97
moral patients 3, 18–20, 25–26, 29,
    32–35, 36, 73, 98, 104
moral perfectionism 7
moral personhood 3, 26, 55–56; *see also*
    personhood
moral philosophy 72, 98–99; African
    3–4, 13; Kant's 107; modern
    European 49
moral property 33, 76n4
moral relationalism 19, 21–22, 40, 71
moral responsibility 21, 26, 32
moral sentimentalism 52–53
moral specialness 26, 35–36
moral status 3–13, 40–56, 59–76; in
    African philosophy 18–38; of
    candidates that cannot use their
    capacities 30–33; concept and
    conception of 21; concept of
    18–25; of dead bodies of 8, 95,
    97, 99–101, 109n1; of dead

human bodies 97–108; defence of 29–37; definition 19–21; degrees of 22–24; empathy and 59–76; empathy-based account of 70; empathy-based interpretation 103–105; human dignity 22–25; human dignity and human rights in modern politics 35–37; of marginal cases 5, 30–31, 36, 71–75; as "modal-relational" approach 70; moral egalitarianism 33–35; moral individualism and relationalism 21–22; partial 102; personhood-based view of 102–103; scepticism and rejection of 25–29; theory of 6–7; *ubuntu* and 40–56; Ubuntu and 59–76; Ubuntu ethics and 40–56, 54–56; Ubuntu thinking on 101–105; Western theories of 99–101; *see also* final good; "full moral status" (FMS)
moral system 48, 52
moral theory(ies) 8, 13n1, 19, 40–41, 45, 52–53, 61, 69–70, 76n2, 98–99, 104, 108; African 8, 104; Afro-communitarian 69; contemporary (sentimentalist) 60; secular 99; Ubuntu-inspired 60; Western 99, 104
moral thought: African 3–4, 29, 42, 46–47, 51, 64–65, 68–69, 72; Confucian 87
moral value(s) 3, 20, 27, 30, 47, 55, 98; *see also* value(s)
moral virtue(s) 44, 53

naturalism 6; ethical 6, 13n4, 20; super- 6, 20
natural kind 74–75
Nussbaum, Martha 99–101; *see also* capabilities approach
Nyerere, Julius 47

okra (soul) 6
ontological capacity(ies) 18, 20–21, 24–30, 33–35, 43, 55, 98, 102–104
other, the 46, 49–50, 61–62, 64, 76n3
"ought implies can" principle 31, 40–42, 54–56, 88

perfectionism 7, 46, 85
perfectionist approach 25, 45–46, 82, 88–89
performance 25, 29, 30, 33, 36–37, 86
personhood 7, 25–29, 30, 32, 35, 36, 43–45, 51, 55–56, 70, 90, 93, 103; African 43; African conception of 25, 27, 45, 93; agent-centred notion of 25, 27–28; -based view of moral status 102–103; capacity-based approach to 29; maximalist approach to 27; meritorious notion of 28; normative concept of 25, 28–29, 55–56, 93; ontological concept of 28; patient-centred notion of 25–26; *see also* moral personhood
philosophy 7, 11, 14n7, 42, 59, 76n4, 86, 99; African 3–6, 8–9, 11–13, 13n4, 13n6, 14n7, 18–38, 42, 54, 68, 81, 88; analytic 11–12, 14n7; analytical 11–12; German 7; "of hell" 50; Western philosophy 3, 6, 22, 25–27, 46, 52; *see also* moral philosophy
political martyrdom 50

rationality 21, 24–28, 37, 72, 74, 87, 89, 100
rational nature 37, 100, 107
relational approaches 22
relationalism 71; *see also* moral relationalism
relationality 63, 67; and empathy 64–65
respect 10, 19, 29–34, 35, 44–45, 51, 85, 92–93, 97, 99–101, 105–108; appraisal 30; recognition 30, 100; unconditional 31
rudimentary psychological characteristics 43

self 46, 49–50, 61, 76n3
self-awareness 20, 25
self-determination 10, 84
selfishness 51; un- 51
self-sacrifice 50–51
sentience 25, 32, 45, 71, 86, 104, 107
severely mentally incapacitated (SMI) 32, 60, 72–74
Smith, Adam 52, 61–62
socialism: African 47

solidarity 44, 69–70, 102
substantial freedoms 100
suffering 8, 37, 81–84, 87, 90, 92–95
sympathy 6, 44, 52–53, 76n1

ubuntu 7–8, 13n5, 40–47, 54–56, 56n1, 56n2, 56n3, 63, 67, 71, 88–89, 93–94, 103, 107–108; as altruism 47–51; as empathy 51–54; *see also* personhood
Ubuntu 7, 11, 13n5, 40–56, 59–76, 76n1, 107; -based account of moral status 13, 40, 42, 54, 56; and euthanasia 87–89; and moral status 40–56, 59–76; *see also ubuntu*; Ubuntu ethics; Ubuntu thinking
Ubuntu ethics 7, 11, 40–56, 59, 63, 69–70, 75; empathy as defining essence of 63–69; and final good and dignity 88–89; and moral status 54–56; and moral status of dead human bodies 97–108; and voluntary euthanasia 81–95; *see also* final good
Ubuntu thinking 8, 12, 18, 29, 41–42, 47, 50, 52, 54, 56, 56n3, 59–60, 63–64, 66–67, 69–70, 75, 76n2, 81–82, 84, 87–92, 95, 97–99, 101, 103–104, 107–108, 109n1
Universal Declaration of Human Rights (UDHR) 35–37
utilitarianism 22

value(s) 10–11, 35, 50–51, 84–85; African 47; agent-centred theory of 29–30; agential account of 102–104; assigning 5–6, 18, 20; capacity-based approach to 3, 5, 21, 26, 29–30, 33, 35–36; complete 28, 103; humane 47; instrumental 28–29, 32, 103; intrinsic 4, 20–21, 28–32, 35, 37, 43, 74–75, 86, 88, 90, 98, 102–103, 106, 108; patient-centred approach to 21, 26, 29; perfectionist theory of 45; self-realization theory of 45; *see also* moral value(s); value theory
value theory 3, 25–30, 36–37; agent-centred approach to 30; capacity-based approach to 29–30, 36; empathy-based account of 81
virtue(s) 44–47, 53; other-regarding 45, 47; pro-social 53; relational 45–48; social 48; *see also* moral virtue(s)
vitality 6, 28, 47, 64
voluntary euthanasia *see* euthanasia

Waldron, Jeremy 22–23, 34
Waldron's hypothesis 22–23
well-being 56n4, 84
Western philosophy 3, 6, 22, 25–27, 46, 52

Yale School of Medicine Cushing Center 105

For Product Safety Concerns and Information please contact our EU
representative GPSR@taylorandfrancis.com
Taylor & Francis Verlag GmbH, Kaufingerstraße 24, 80331 München, Germany

www.ingramcontent.com/pod-product-compliance
Lightning Source LLC
Chambersburg PA
CBHW051755230426
43670CB00012B/2291